10/28/15

COME FOLLOW ME

Ramon —
For friendship
& faith!
Bill

COME FOLLOW ME

William C. Mills

OCABS PRESS
ST PAUL, MINNESOTA 55124
2015

COME FOLLOW ME

ISBN 1-60191-032-0

PRINTED IN THE UNITED STATES OF AMERICA

Come Follow Me

ISBN 1-60191-032-0

Published by OCABS Press, St. Paul, Minnesota.
Printed in the United States of America.

Books are available through OCABS Press at special discounts for bulk purchases in the United States by academic institutions, churches, and other organizations. For more information please email OCABS Press at press@ocabs.org.

Cover: Walters Ms. W592, Gospels. fol. 261b. Jesus blessing the children.

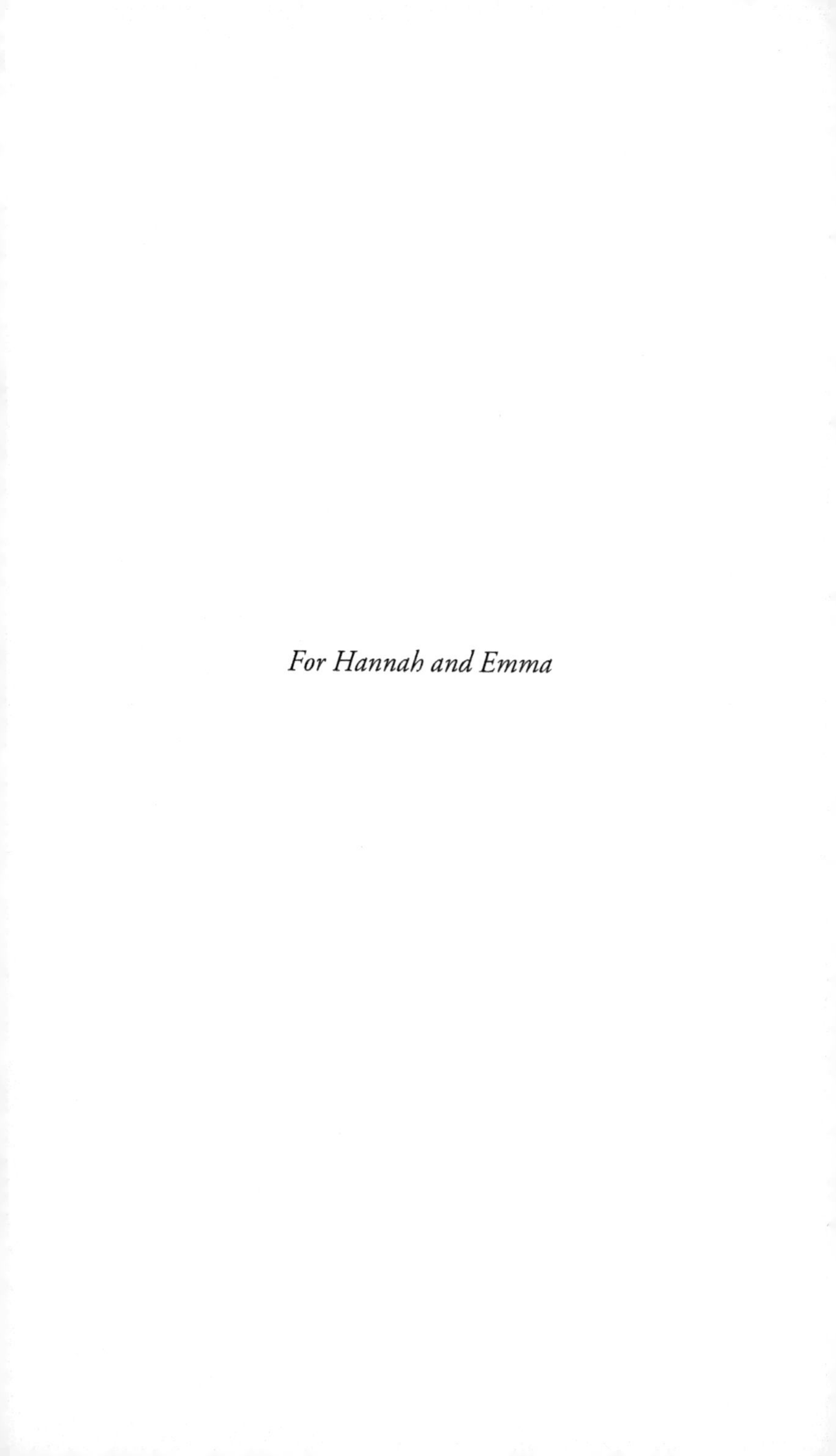

For Hannah and Emma

Table of Contents

Introduction

One day Jesus walked along the Sea of Galilee and saw Andrew, Peter, James, and John. He called them with three simple words: come follow me. They dropped their nets and followed. They dropped their way of life and followed. They dropped what was familiar and followed. They didn't ask where they were going or what they should bring or what they'll be doing, but they followed.

The disciples were fishermen. They were familiar with nets, boats, bait, hooks, weather patterns, buying, and selling, but they knew nothing of preaching, teaching, and ministering. They knew nothing of healing. Their life revolved around fishing and the fishing industry. Yet Jesus' call changed them. They followed Jesus from Jericho to Jerusalem, from Tyre to Sidon, and from Bethany and beyond. Their world in Bethsaida was very small, but when Jesus called their lives were enlarged and enriched. They met soldiers and tax collectors, rich and poor, Jew and Gentile. One day they were fishermen, the next day they became fishers of men. For two thousand years people have been changed by those three simple words: come follow me.

Come Follow Me is a collection of pastoral reflections on select Bible passages that will hopefully inspire you to deepen your faith in the one who called the first disciples and who also calls us. Jesus calls us to leave behind what is comfortable, to leave what we hold near and dear and follow him into the deep dark mystery of life. Jesus calls us to unchartered territories, away from our comfort zone, where we meet the stranger and the sojourner. Ultimately he calls us to carry our cross as we make our daily walk of faith.

There will be days when we don't want to follow. There will be days when we follow easily and eagerly. There will be days when we get tired and don't want to take another step. Yet Jesus still calls us with three simple words: come follow me. Hopefully we will.

Each chapter begins with a short Scripture passage. Read the short commentary and allow the words to deepen your understanding of the Scriptural text. Then at the end, take some quiet time to answer the food for thought questions that will assist you in your faith journey.

Chapter One

Faith Not Fear

Jesus left that place and went away to the district of Tyre and Sidon. Just then a Canaanite woman from that region came out and started shouting, "Have mercy on me, Lord, Son of David; my daughter is tormented by a demon." But he did not answer her at all. And his disciples came and urged him, saying, "Send her away, for she keeps shouting after us." He answered, "I was sent only to the lost sheep of the house of Israel." But she came and knelt before him, saying, "Lord, help me." He answered, "It is not fair to take the children's food and throw it to the dogs." She said, "Yes, Lord, yet even the dogs eat the crumbs that fall from their masters' table." Then Jesus answered her, "Woman, great is your faith! Let it be done for you as you wish." And her daughter was healed instantly (Matthew 15:21-28).

A few years ago I visited a friend in New York. He told me that he couldn't pick me up at the airport entrance but that he'd wait in the cell phone lot and wait for my call. After debarking from the plane I reached into my backpack and noticed that my cell phone needed charging. I looked around but couldn't find an available outlet. One lady had her computer hooked up in one and someone else had an iPad in the other. The only available outlet was next to the restroom. I walked over and plugged in the phone. I waited for a moment then tried calling. Nothing. I unplugged the phone and walked outside hoping that my friend might be waiting. He wasn't there. I returned back inside and plugged the phone into the wall again. After a few minutes I still couldn't make a call so I walked back outside. On my left I saw a sign: cell phone lot. I started walking. It was a bitterly cold March evening. After walking a few yards I noticed a taxi driver sitting in his car. I motioned for him to roll down his window and asked how far the cell lot was. He said about one or two miles up the road. I wasn't going to walk two miles in the freezing cold.

While all of this was going on, a man stood at the curbside waiting for his ride. He must have noticed me going in and out of the terminal and asked, "Are you okay?" I said, "Yeah, I'm fine." I paused for a moment then told him the story about my phone. He reached out and offered me his cell. "No, it's okay," I said, "I'll just wait. My friend is going to pick me up soon." He asked, "Are you sure?" I waved my head no. The cold wind tore through me. I wasn't used to the northern winter. A few moments later I said, "Would you mind if I borrow your phone and call my friend?" I called and a few minutes later my friend came and picked me up.

Unlike the woman in the gospel I was too proud to ask for help.

The woman was bold and brazen. She marched right up to Jesus and asked for help. You might ask yourself, so what, a lot of people approached Jesus for help, why is this any different?

This unnamed woman had three strikes against her. First, she was a woman and women were forbidden to approach a rabbi. Second, she was a Canaanite and in the Old Testament the Canaanites were bitter enemies of the

Israelites. Third, she was from the region of Tyre and Sidon which was Gentile territory. Back then Jews and Gentiles didn't mix. This woman never let race or religion prevent her from approaching Jesus. She wasn't afraid. She asked for help.

In the Sermon on the Mount, Jesus says; "Ask, and it will be given to you; seek, and you will find; knock, and it will be opened to you" (Matthew 7:7). Do we ask, seek, and knock? My hunch is that we don't. Most of the time we're too afraid. Fear is an obstacle to faith. Fear prevents us from approaching Jesus. Fear is powerful.

In the 1960's and 70's sociologists were studying how people help others. The researchers performed an experiment in three places: on a college campus, on the side of a road, and on a major highway. They hired an actor to play a victim. The actor was told to curl up on the ground and act distressed. They were told not to interact with anyone.

The researchers hid behind bushes and watched. One passerby noticed the actor on the ground and then walked by. Another person walked over to him, looked, and then walked away. Yet another passerby stopped, talked with him, and then walked away. Hours went by before someone actually stopped and called for help. At the end of the experiment the researchers approached those who passed by and asked why they didn't help the actor. They all responded the same way: they were afraid to get involved. They were afraid to call for the police or the EMT. They were afraid of lawsuits or fights with the family. Fear prevented them from helping someone in need.

Fear is powerful. It prevents us from being bold and brazen like the woman in the gospel. I hope that we can all have a little more faith than fear as we follow Jesus every day.

Food For Thought

1. The Canaanite woman was an outsider yet she was not afraid to ask for help. Have you had similar situations when you were afraid to ask for help when you needed it?

2. The Canaanite woman probably suffered from a lot of shame and social stigma. Yet she didn't allow her shame from preventing her from approaching Jesus. Social stigma is very powerful. Have you ever encountered social stigma in your life? What were the circumstances? How did you overcome it?

3. Read: Ruth 1:1-10, Luke 18:1-8, Psalm 23

Chapter Two

It Takes a Village

News of this came to the ears of the church in Jerusalem, and they sent Barnabas to Antioch. When he came and saw the grace of God, he rejoiced, and he exhorted them all to remain faithful to the Lord with steadfast devotion; for he was a good man, full of the Holy Spirit and of faith. And a great many people were brought to the Lord. Then Barnabas went to Tarsus to look for Saul, and when he had found him, he brought him to Antioch. So it was that for an entire year they met with the church and taught a great many people, and it was in Antioch that the disciples were first called "Christians." (Acts 11:22-24)

There is an African proverb that says it takes a village to raise a child.

Whether you're from a single or two-parent household raising a family is hard work. I grew up in a nuclear American family: mom, dad, and myself. We rarely had visitors except maybe for Thanksgiving, Christmas, or Easter.

My family was the opposite of Anthony's family. Anthony was Filipino and his house was like Grand Central Station. Anthony had a mom, dad, brother, sister, aunt, and grandmother all living under the same roof. After I finished my homework I'd run down to Anthony's house and we'd watch television together in the living room. His grandma would occasionally peek her head out of the kitchen. She couldn't speak English so she just stood there smiling at me and I'd smile back. A few minutes later his aunt, who also couldn't speak English, would wave at me and I'd wave back. The house was loud and boisterous and always smelled like onions, garlic, and fish.

Even though Anthony attended an American school and had American friends, his parents didn't seem worried about losing their Filipino culture. Even though Anthony spoke English at school he spoke Tagalog at home. His parents didn't seem worried about him loosing his faith either. Anthony's family was Catholic and they attended St. Joseph's Catholic Church which was just down the block from his house. They all walked to Church on Sunday. If his parents couldn't go his aunt would take them. If his aunt couldn't go his grandma would take them. One of the biggest problems immigrants face is loosing their language, faith, and culture. It's so hard to maintain all of this if there is no social or communal support.

It takes a village to raise a child.

When reading the Book of Acts we see that wherever Paul traveled he spent quite a bit of time in each location. He spent three weeks in Athens. He spent a year in Antioch. He spent a year and a half in Corinth. Luke isn't specific, but when we read the rest of Acts we know that Paul preached to them, taught them the gospel, and most likely ate with them, laughed with them, and cried with them. What do you do when you visit a friend or a family member for long periods of time? You become part of their family, you follow their schedule, you eat what they eat and do what they do. In other words Paul and Barnabas became part of the Corinthian Christian family.

Evangelism takes time. We think that we can snap our fingers and folks will flock to us. Others think that we can put up a Facebook account or flashy website and people will want to join our congregations. It doesn't work that way. Pastoral care and ministry takes time. It takes time to build relationships and allow seekers to find their way in their new spiritual home. It isn't something that we do overnight. It isn't something that takes a day or a week or a month. It takes a lifetime of prayerful patience and hopeful expectation.

Food For Thought

1. People join a parish community not because of the physical plant or whether or not the parish has a bell tower or fancy artwork, they join because they want meaningful worship and an intentional community based on love. Rather than put ads in the paper or spend money for flyers maybe we should focus our time and energy on creating vibrant communities of faith?

2. The spiritual life is more like a marathon than a sprint. Paul spent eighteen months in Corinth building up the Church. Eighteen months is a long time. Take the long view rather than the short-term view of things. Discipleship is a long haul and you must maintain balance along the way.

3. Read: Matthew 10:1-15, Romans 10:1-17, Acts 6:1-10

Chapter Three

Turn Like a Child

"I am the good shepherd. The good shepherd lays down his life for the sheep. The hired hand, who is not the shepherd and does not own the sheep, sees the wolf coming and leaves the sheep and runs away—and the wolf snatches them and scatters them. The hired hand runs away because a hired hand does not care for the sheep. I am the good shepherd. I know my own and my own know me, just as the Father knows me and I know the Father. And I lay down my life for the sheep. I have other sheep that do not belong to this fold. I must bring them also, and they will listen to my voice. So there will be one flock, one shepherd. (John 10:9-16)

We know that Jesus wasn't married and therefore didn't have a family of his own, but he certainly knew a lot about children. When we encounter children we may think they're cute and cuddly, but that's not always the case. We think that children are cherubs but that's not true either. More often than not children can be little devils.

Jesus said two important things about children, "Let the children come to me, and do not hinder them; for such belongs the kingdom of heaven" (Matthew 19:14) and "But whoever causes one of these little ones who believes in me to sin, it would be better for him to have a great millstone fastened around his neck and be drowned in the depths of the sea." (Matthew 18:6). A millstone was a large stone used for grinding wheat, flax, and other grains. It was so large that a donkey or a horse had to be tied to a wooden beam so that the millstone could be turned.

Jesus used children as an example because he was familiar with children and how they think. When you read the gospels you will notice that Jesus didn't use fancy words or concepts but simple everyday examples like bread, oil, fire, water, wine, and sheep and shepherds to name a few.

There was a woman named Sofia Cavalletti.[78] Sofia had a doctorate in New Testament and taught Scriptures in a college in Rome. After Mass one day the priest walked over to her and asked, "Sofia, I need someone to teach Church school. I know you have a family and kids and teach at the college. You'll be a great addition to our teaching staff." Sofia said, "But Father, I teach college students, not children. He said, "Yes I know Sofa but I need help." She said, "Okay, I'll try it." So she did.

The next Sunday Sofia walked into the class. She said, "Ok, today is going to be an easy lesson." She read a passage from the gospel of John three times. The first time she read it in a regular voice. The second time she read it slower and the third time she read it even slower, pausing between each stanza. Then she said, "Ok, here's some paper. You can draw anything you wish for the next forty-

---

[78] Sofia Cavaletti is an important figure in contemporary Christian Education and the creator of the popular *Catechesis of the Good Shepherd* that is used in the Catholic Church. See also Sofia Cavaletti and Patricia Coulter (trans.) *The Religious Potential of the Child* 2nd ed. (Chicago: Liturgical Training Publications, 1992).

five minutes. At eleven o'clock we'll stop." A little boy raised his hand and asked, "You mean we can draw anything?" She said, "Yes, anything you wish." So they started drawing. Sofia walked around the room. She was surprised at what she saw.

The first boy had a picture of Jesus and some sheep. She asked the boy about the picture. The boy said that it was Jesus leading the sheep. Then a little girl had a picture of Jesus and the sheep in front of him. Sofia asked why Jesus was facing the sheep and the girl said that Jesus was teaching the sheep. Another picture had Jesus in the middle of the page. The boy was counting the other children in the class and then looking down at his picture and then looking up again. She walked over and saw that Jesus was in the middle of the picture and there were sheep all round him in a circle, each one had a name: Antonio, Maria, Carla, and so forth. Sofia asked why all of the sheep had names and the boy said that Jesus calls each one of us by name. Then a little girl had a picture of Jesus on the cross and next to him with a large candle and the sheep were all gathered around him. Sofia asked the little girl what her picture was about and the little girl said that she heard her priest say that Jesus is the light of the world and that he leads us to the cross, and as the sheep we follow him. Finally a little girl had a picture of an Altar table with a cup and a saucer and a man behind it and the sheep all around it. Sofia asked what is this about and the girl said, "Oh that's our priest. Jesus feeds us with the bread and the wine every Sunday and as the Good Shepherd he feeds us too." All of the children were between four and eight years old.

Turn Like a Child

Jesus taught people using simple terms and concepts; simple but not simplistic. Unfortunately we often make simple things complicated. Jesus offers us the simplest thing: life itself. Not just life, but His Life. Every Sunday Jesus invites us to his table where we eat bread and wine. We eat the food of eternal life yet we keep choosing other things instead. He still offers us life in abundance and yet we keep choosing the things of this world. We keep choosing things that are not good for us. He offers things that build up and encourage and we keep choosing things that will destroy and hurt. The book of Deuteronomy says that there are two ways: the way that leads to destruction and death and the way that leads to life (Deuteronomy 30:15). I hope that we can all choose life.

Food For Thought

1. Sofia was comfortable teaching adults but not children. Her priest saw gifts in her that she had but didn't recognize. Our life journey is one of self-discovery, seeking to unpack the many gifts, talents, and treasures that God has given us. Take some time and look at your life. Maybe you have gifts and talents that you aren't using at the moment but could be using? Life is short; we must use all of our gifts for the glory of God.

2. Adults think that children don't pay attention in Church. Yet children learn a lot during worship. They can see candles, incense, artwork, and colors. They hear music. Each week these sacred

symbols are repeated and reinforced so that over time the child will come to a deeper knowledge of faith. Your job as parents is to bring them to Church so that they can learn.

3. Read: Psalm 127, Proverbs 17, Matthew 19:9-13

Chapter Four

You Give Them Something to Eat

Now when Jesus heard this, he withdrew from there in a boat to a deserted place by himself. But when the crowds heard it, they followed him on foot from the towns. When he went ashore, he saw a great crowd; and he had compassion for them and cured their sick. When it was evening, the disciples came to him and said, "This is a deserted place, and the hour is now late; send the crowds away so that they may go into the villages and buy food for themselves." Jesus said to them, "They need not go away; you give them something to eat." (Matthew 14:13-25)

Summer means cookouts and family gatherings. A family invited some friends for a cookout. They were going to have a simple meal: hotdogs, hamburgers, potato and macaroni salad. Earlier in the day the family said, "Oh, by the way. Would you mind if we brought my mother-in-law? She's living with us and we didn't think you'd mind." "No problem," they said, "We have a few extra hamburgers around." Then the family said, "Oh, would you mind then if we bring my brother, his wife, and three adult children? They just popped in and surprised us. We didn't know whether or not they were welcome?" The wife did what I usually do, she gritted her teeth and said, "Yes, of course, no problem at all." And then she sent her husband to the store to get some more hotdogs. She was not a happy camper.

You might think that this type of thing only happens to other people. That's what I thought until it happened to me. One year while I was working as the seminary cook I had to prepare a lunch for a group of folks who attended our annual Lenten retreat. We planned a lunch for about a hundred people. I was going to make pasta salad, a five-bean salad, hummus and pita bread, and some fresh fruit for dessert. After spending most of the morning in the kitchen I sat down for a coffee break. My feet hurt and I was tired. It was almost lunchtime and the student workers delivered food to the chapel basement. After the students left my boss came into the kitchen and said, "We have a little problem."

In the food industry there's no such thing as a little problem. A little problem is always a big problem. "You made extra food, right?" She said. "Of course I made extra food." I replied. "Oh, good. I just wanted you to know have about thirty extra people coming. They just called and they'll be in time for lunch." I looked at her and at the clock and in the best of my Christian charity said, "Why can't they go down to one of those restaurants on Central Avenue?" She said, "Well, they can, but they paid for the retreat and for the lunch so we need to feed them." I looked at her for a moment, let out a big sigh, finished my coffee, and walked over to the fridge, got some extra onions, peppers, and cucumbers and started preparing food for thirty extra people. It was one of those days when I wish I weren't a Christian.

I'm pretty sure the disciples may have felt like I did that day when Jesus told them to feed that great big crowd. Matthew says that Jesus stopped at that particular place because everyone was tired. The disciples were probably hungry and thirsty and I could imagine them telling Jesus, "Can't you send the crowds away?" Jesus looks at them and says, "You give them something to eat." They probably said, "Jesus, we're tired." He says, "You give them something to eat." Peter complains about his bunions and bursitis and Jesus still says, "You give them something to eat." Andrew says he's a fisherman, not a cook, yet Jesus says, "You give them something to eat." The disciples look around at the crowds and there are more of them than there are disciples. Jesus still tells them, "You give them something to eat." They say, "But Lord, we only have five small loaves and two fish here, can't they go down the road to the deli or something?" Jesus says, "You give them something to eat." The disciples are overwhelmed. Finally the disciples stop complaining and bring Jesus five small loaves and two fish. He breaks and blesses them and gives them to the people. Not only are they fed and filled but there are leftovers too. Jesus knows what he's doing.

Jesus invited the disciples to feed the world. Today we are invited to feed the world too. We look around and like the disciples find reasons not to do it. We're tired. We're aggravated. We have other things to do. Yet Jesus tells us, "You give them something to eat."

When we hear these words we may feel like we're not qualified either. Feeding people may not be in our skill set. Yet in the Bible we find there's a host of people who weren't qualified either: Moses stuttered, Abraham was old, Isaac was a dreamer, Jacob was a cheater, David had an affair, Noah got drunk, Elisha was suicidal, Jonah ran from God, Gideon was insecure, Miriam was a gossiper, Sarah was impatient, Elijah was moody, Rehab was a prostitute, Samson liked prostitutes, Isaiah was crazy, Jeremiah was emotional, Martha was a worrier, Peter had a temper, John the Baptist was eccentric, James and John argued, Judas was greedy, Thomas was a doubter, Paul was a murderer, Timothy was sickly, Zacchaeus was short. We could easily find more people in the Bible that would fit into one of those categories too.

I'm sure most of us can identify with one or more of the people and their problems. We make excuses why we don't want to follow or why it's too hard. None of us are qualified, yet God still calls each and every one of us. He calls us to us as he did the disciples, "You give them something to eat."

Food For Thought

1. Take some quiet time alone and look at your life. What are your excuses for not following Jesus? Make a list. In your daily prayer ask Jesus to open your heart and use all of your gifts for his glory.

2. The Church is a refuge for the poor. Jesus fed five thousand people in one day. While we can't feed five thousand people maybe we can feed five? Fifteen? Many parishes host food banks or soup kitchens. Maybe you can get involved and

start feeding people. Jesus feeds us so we can feed others.

3. Read: John 6:1-30, Romans 1:1-10, Matthew 10:1-15.

Chapter Five

Lazarus at My Door

"There was a rich man who was dressed in purple and fine linen and who feasted sumptuously every day. And at his gate lay a poor man named Lazarus, covered with sores, who longed to satisfy his hunger with what fell from the rich man's table; even the dogs would come and lick his sores. The poor man died and was carried away by the angels to be with Abraham." (Luke 16:19-22)

One night our family was downtown watching a play. While walking back to our car I noticed two guys lying on a park bench looking as if they were preparing for sleep. One of the guys was wrapped in a blanket. A passerby might have thought they were on drugs or drunk or mentally ill.

While driving home later that night I realized that I live in a social bubble. When I get my mail I don't see people in my driveway and when I go to the store I don't see homeless people in the street. I don't see folks outside on a cold winter night. We get up in the morning, we go to work, and we return home. For the most part the poor are invisible.

A few years ago I met a single mother. She was nicely dressed and if you saw her on the street you couldn't tell what type of job she had. After dropping off her son at school she went to work and then at four o'clock picked him up, fed him supper, dropped him off at a neighbor's house and went to night school. After her evening class she picked up her son from the nanny and drove home. When

I talked with her I asked where she worked and she said she worked at the Salvation Army. She said that she worked there as a way to thank them for everything they did for her. She later told me that for a while she lived in her car, on friends' couches and floors, and then finally she saved enough money to rent a small apartment for both herself and her son. Yet when I saw her that day I had no idea that she was homeless. For all intents and purposes she was just like Lazarus.

We probably encounter many more Lazarus' in our life then we think. And these Lazarus' are not lying on the side of the road nor begging for money or hanging out in front of homes or dumpster diving; no, these Lazarus' look like you and me. They're usually nicely dressed and educated and they don't smell like vomit and urine. No, these Lazarus' look normal yet they're poor.

The Lazarus' in my life are always broken and in pain. Jesus reminds us in the Sermon on the Mount, "Blessed are the poor in spirit, for theirs is the Kingdom of Heaven." Yes, they are broken. Yes they are grieving. Yes they are dealing with all sorts of problems and pain, addictions, and doubts. They are like Lazarus begging for a cup of cool water and food for the journey. It's our choice whether to help them or not.

I encounter Lazarus in my neighborhood, at the grocery store, in my family, and in my parish. I am reminded of Lazarus every time I come to Church and see the Loaves and Fishes bins and wonder when will there be a time when I don't have to remind people to donate canned food. I am reminded of Lazarus every time I see the

Florence Crittendon bins and wonder when can we stop donating diapers to single mothers. I am reminded of Lazarus when every November we adopt our angels for Christmas and wonder when will there be a time when we don't have to buy gifts for poor children anymore. Yes, Lazarus is among us, if we just have the eyes to see.

It's been my experience that Lazarus wants something more precious than money. He wants my time. It's easy to give someone ten dollars for lunch, but its much harder to sit and listen to them pour out their hearts about their pains and problems. It's much easier to give them a sandwich and say, "God be with you" than to sit and eat with them as you offer compassion and consolation.

I know someone who works at an Episcopal Church in San Francisco. Monday through Friday from eleven to one o'clock they serve a hot lunch for the homeless. After lunch they are invited to take a bag of canned food home with them, some soup and vegetables and fruits. Every day she arrives by nine o'clock and people are already lining up for lunch. They're not always peaceful either. One day she noticed a Russian and a Korean lady arguing over the last head of cabbage. They both wanted it but neither wanted to share. My friend said she wish she had a knife and cut the cabbage in half just to make them both happy.

Loving Lazarus can be frustrating and almost impossible, yet it's the Jesus way. I hope the next time you encounter Lazarus, whether it's this week, this month, or this year, that you give him what he needs. Our salvation depends on it.

Food For Thought

1. Take some time and think about the Lazarus' in your life. They can be in your family, in your neighborhood, in your parish, or at work. Keep these people in prayer and think of ways to help them towards wholeness and healing.

2. We are often blind to peoples' pains and problems. It's easy to neglect caring for those right under our roofs. Take some time this week and be extra special loving to those around you. Jesus reminds us that the greatest command in the Bible is to love God with all your heart, soul, strength, and mind and your neighbor as yourself. Our salvation depends on our love of the neighbor.

3. Read: Matthew 25:31:46, Isaiah 58:1-14, Acts 6:1-7

Chapter Six

Them Dry Bones

The hand of the Lord came upon me, and he brought me out by the spirit of the Lord and set me down in the middle of a valley; it was full of bones. He led me all around them; there were very many lying in the valley, and they were very dry. He said to me, "Mortal, can these bones live?" I answered, "O Lord God, you know." Then he said to me, "Prophesy to these bones, and say to them: O dry bones, hear the word of the Lord. Thus says the Lord God to these bones: I will cause breath to enter you, and you shall live. I will lay sinews on you, and will cause flesh to come upon you, and cover you with skin, and put breath in you, and you shall live; and you shall know that I am the Lord." (Ezekiel 37:1-6)

I always liked this particular reading from Ezekiel. I say particular because most of Ezekiel is pretty scary especially the beginning chapters when he talks about strange figures whirling and twirling around and the Spirit leaving the temple. It reminds me of science fiction fantasy. However I still find Ezekiel's worlds comforting.

There have been times in life when I felt like that valley of dry bones: dry, dusty, and distressed. There have been times in my life when I felt like there was no more life in me. No blood circulating through my veins. No breath in my lungs. Nothing. I'm sure that you too may have had one or two of these dry periods. If not, you haven't lived. There are times when you might feel like there's no more life in you. You put one foot in front of the other but you don't feel like you're getting anywhere. You move ahead through the vast desert of life. You might even feel like these dry dead bones that Ezekiel speaks about.

Ezekiel's prophecy came around the same time as the return of the Israelites from their exile in Babylon. King Nebuchadnezzar had captured Jerusalem and exiled all the Israelites to Babylon, the capital of the Babylonian Empire. There, as we read in Psalm 137, they sat down and wept and hung their lyres and harps on willow trees and remembered how good they had it back in Jerusalem. They had a hard time singing the Lord's song in a foreign land. Ezekiel says that they were like the dry ones, there was no longer any life in them. They were cut off from their lifeline.

Yet God is always good. While reading the prophets I'm amazed how often the Israelites rebelled against God. They're worse than a bunch of teenagers; self centered, lazy, and always complaining. Yet God never forgets them. God never ceases to forgive them. God never stops loving them. As God told Ezekiel, "I will cause breath to enter you, and you shall live. I will lay sinews on you, and will cause flesh to come upon you, and cover you with skin, and put breath in you, and you shall live; and you shall know that I am the Lord." Those are comforting words. God's breath will come and will enliven them. He will give them flesh and muscles and make them alive and well. Once they were dead and nearly buried and now they will be alive. But Ezekiel reminds them that its not their doing, its God's doing.

This passage reminds me of the opening portion of Genesis. God takes the simple dry dust from the earth and like a potter shapes Adam. Genesis says that God breathed life into him. In John's gospel we hear that after his resurrection, Jesus' breathed on his disciples too, he says "Peace be unto you" (John 20:21). The risen Lord breathes upon his disciples and gives them them life. They are sent out into the world to continue Jesus' ministry, "Jesus said to them again, "Peace be with you. As the Father has sent me, so I send you." When he had said this, he breathed on them and said to them, "Receive the Holy Spirit." I find that comforting. This same spirit that God breathed into Adam in Genesis and which hovered upon the chaotic waters is now given to the disciples. Surely the disciples were scared, confused, angry, and upset when they saw their Lord and friend arrested, put on trial, arrested, and put to death. Yet even after all of this he gives them the Holy Spirit. The risen Lord comes to us too and breathes life into us, giving us new life to our old tired bones.

Food For Thought

1. Have there been times when you felt dry and tired? Our culture puts much more emphasis on production, not persons. We are valued more for what we produce than on who we are in the eyes of God. An essential part of our walk of faith is Sabbath rest. Take some time away by yourself. Maybe take a walk, work in the garden, or read a portion of the Bible. You might think all of this is wasting time, but you will find yourself renewed and rejuvenated.

2. God breathed life into the dry bones in the desert. God breathes life into us as well. Genesis says that God breathed life into Adam. Take some time and reflect on the great gift of life. Every day is a gift from God. Savor each and every moment as a great gift of grace.

3. Read: Jeremiah 2:6-10, Isaiah 58:11-13, Matthew 13:6

Chapter Seven

Letting Go

Then he led them out as far as Bethany, and, lifting up his hands, he blessed them. While he was blessing them, he withdrew from them and was carried up into heaven. And they worshiped him, and returned to Jerusalem with great joy; and they were continually in the temple blessing God. (Luke 24:50-53)

In May 1995 I began a ten-week summer internship at St. Stephen's Orthodox parish in Orlando, Florida. My job was to assist the pastor. On some days I went with him on hospital visits and on other days I prepared weekly sermons. I sang in the choir and wrote the Sunday bulletin. I was excited. It was my first taste of parish life.

However I became quickly disappointed. In my home parish we had pews, St. Stephen's had a few chairs along the back wall. In my home parish they had stained glass windows decorated with biblical scenes. St. Stephen's had plain windows. In my home parish we used *trespasses* in the Lord's Prayer. St. Stephen's they used *debts and debtors*. But the biggest difference was the men. In my home parish men wore shirts, ties, and sports jackets. But at St. Stephen's they wore polo shirts or dress shirts with no ties or jackets. I was scandalized. How dare they come to Church half dressed? I thought these guys were barbarians.

After a few weeks I came to experience that these folks were really nice. They welcomed me into their homes. They invited me over for dinner. They patiently listened to my sermons and attended Bible studies. At the end of the summer they gave me a beautiful icon of St. Stephen. They were warm and welcoming but I didn't realize how arrogant and judgmental I was. I thought that I knew everything about the Church. I thought that my job was to teach them. I learned many lessons that summer, most of which you can't learn from a lecture or read from a textbook. I had to let a lot of things go that summer.

Letting go is not easy. Letting go can be painful.

The Ascension is about letting go. Luke tells us that on the first Easter Sunday Cleopas and another unnamed disciple were on their way to Emmaus, a small village about seven miles from Jerusalem. While walking they met a man whom they don't know. He asked Cleopas what was wrong, why did he look so down. Cleopas tells him, don't you know? That Jesus the Christ has been crucified? Don't you know that a great prophet has died? Then after a while this stranger teaches them the scriptures and then they stop to eat. Luke tells us that this person took bread and blessed it. Then he took wine and gave thanks. Afterwards Luke says that their hearts burned within them and that he was known to them in the breaking of the bread. We eventually come to know that this unnamed sojourner was the risen Lord.

Cleopas was clearly upset. After all, his friend has just died. He was anxious because he didn't know what else to do. He was probably angry because for three years he followed Jesus and now there was no one to guide and lead them. Cleopas had to let all of that go. Jesus told them don't worry, wait in Jerusalem until the Spirit comes.

John's gospel reports that on the first Easter morning Mary Magdalene came to the tomb and was preparing to anoint Jesus' dead body with spices, but instead she encountered a gardener. The gardener was really Jesus but she didn't know that. He turns and calls her name: Mary. She recognizes his voice. She called out Rabboni which is Aramaic for Rabbi. He says, "Mary, don't touch me. Don't cling to me. Don't hold onto me, For I must go to your father and to my father, to your God and to my God." What kind of greeting is that? Mary missed Jesus. She was excited to see him again yet he tells her, don't touch me, don't cling to me, don't hold onto me. If I don't go to my Father and to your Father, to my God and your God, the Spirit won't come. If the Spirit doesn't come then he will not guide you or lead you or show you the way.

When I was young I used to visit my uncle Irv and Aunt Joanne. Aunt Joanne wore black and looked downcast all the time. She didn't leave the house very often. I asked my father why Aunt Joanne was like that and he told me a story.

One night Aunt Joanne's daughter Cynthia was driving home with a few friends and the car crashed. A few of her friends survived, but Cynthia didn't. Counselors and therapists say that we need to work through our grief. After time passes, when all the hurt and pain are gone you move on. You continue to live. Aunt Joanne never got on with life. She never let go of her daughter.

Richard Rohr is a Franciscan priest and author. He says that there are two halves of life; the first half is from birth to around forty. The second half goes from forty to the time of death. The first half of life is primarily focused on gathering and collecting. Children collect toys, games, books, rocks, and clothes. Young adults collect friends, money, and material things. Older adults collect homes, cars, and pensions. Rohr says, a mature Christian needs to come to terms what really matters in life. The second half of life is about letting go. It's about letting go of all the clutter, even spiritual and religious clutter in our lives that gets in the way of fully living in the Spirit. Letting go of our garbage that hinders us from living a full life in Christ.

You might want to ask yourself: What do I have to let go of? Maybe you have to let go of anger? Maybe you have to let go of toxic friendships or relationships that aren't helpful or wholesome? Maybe you need to let go of some dreams that you now realize will never materialize? Maybe you need to let go of material things that you keep collecting and collecting and it bogs you down?

As a pastor I've had to let go of lots of people; some because of death and others who moved away. Letting go, even for me, isn't easy. Letting go is difficult because you build relationships with folks. You hear their confessions. You share meals. You have a life together. When they leave its hard. But I've learned that just as Mary let go of Jesus, so too we must let go.

Food For Thought

1. Take some time and make a list of all the things that you had to let go of. Read over each one and

write down a few sentences about each one. How do you feel about these items?

2. Do you still have a hard time letting go? Why do you think this is?

3. Read: Proverbs 3:5-6, Ephesians 4:31-2, Philippians 3:12-14

Chapter Eight

A New Era

Then Jesus, filled with the power of the Spirit, returned to Galilee, and a report about him spread through all the surrounding country. He began to teach in their synagogues and was praised by everyone. When he came to Nazareth, where he had been brought up, he went to the synagogue on the Sabbath day, as was his custom. He stood up to read, and the scroll of the prophet Isaiah was given to him. He unrolled the scroll and found the place where it was written: "The Spirit of the Lord is upon me, because he has anointed me to bring good news to the poor. He has sent me to proclaim release to the captives and recovery of sight to the blind, to let the oppressed go free, to proclaim the year of the Lord's favor." And he rolled up the scroll, gave it back to the attendant, and sat down. The eyes of all in the synagogue were fixed on him. Then he began to say to them, "Today this scripture has been fulfilled in your hearing." (Luke 4:14-21)

There's so much tragedy taking place in the world today. This year thousands of innocent men, women, and children were forced out of their homes in Mosul, Iraq, which was at one time a Christian town and now only has a handful of believers. Or the ongoing fighting in the Ukraine between the Russian separatists who bombed both homes and churches. And then there is the perennial problems in Gaza where nearly two thousand innocent people have been killed in senseless fighting. One reporter said that they call all the residents in the apartment building and give them an hour to leave. The military calls at least three times to make sure they get the message. And then, as promised, after an hour they bomb the building. Everything is destroyed. The people have nowhere to live. Hundreds of homeless families have to share food, clothing, and shelter.

When I heard about this I wondered what things would I take if I were given one hour to leave. Probably my computer, some pictures, a few books, maybe some important papers, and of course my family and the pets. But one hour isn't much time. I was never forced to leave my home, forced to leave my culture, forced to leave my faith. I was never forced to pack up and get out of town never to return again. But Isaiah did.

Isaiah lived during the time of the Babylonian exile and watched as the Israelites were rounded up and forced to leave Jerusalem. They too, like the poor peasants in Gaza and Mosul packed up their bags and left all that was near and dear to them. They had to leave their lives behind and travel across a vast desert to a foreign land. Their daughters had to marry foreign men. They had to leave their food and culture behind. The Lord sent the prophet Isaiah to remind the Israelites that He still loved them. Isaiah was sent to bring them the good news of salvation, to open the eyes of the blind, and to set free those who were captive.

I've led a privileged life. Yet there have been times in my life when I've felt very lonely, so lonely that I felt that no one cared about me. But when I stopped and thought about it I remembered that God still loved me in my loneliness.

Even though I can physically see and everything is okay with my eyes there were times in my life when I was blind, when I couldn't distinguish between the forest from the trees. I felt like I was surrounded by darkness. Yet God opened my eyes to see. I've never been in prison yet I've felt like I've been captive to things that held me back from following the Lord.

Jesus told the people sitting in the synagogue that Isaiah's words were fulfilled in their hearing. Those same words are fulfilled in our hearing too. Jesus is our messiah, our savior who opens the eyes of the blind, who releases the captives and who preaches good news to the poor.

Food For Thought

1. Take some quiet time and think of all the times when you felt like you were in darkness or perhaps were in an emotional or spiritual prison. How did you feel? How does it feel now that you are different? Maybe you are still being held captive by past events or bad memories? Remember that God loves you and wants you to be free. As St. Paul says in his letter to the Galatians that for freedom Christ has set us free (Galatians 5:13). Use this Scripture verse as your prayer during the coming days and weeks and see where it leads you.

2. A big part of following Jesus is reading and listening to his words. We won't know our faith

unless we learn it first. Take a few minutes each day and read a selection from Scripture. I suggest that you start with the Psalms. The Psalms are poetry and most of them are rather short. Read a Psalm a day, take time for reflection, and then go about your business. After a while the words will become a part of you.

3. Read: James 1:19, Titus 3:2, Luke 4:1

Chapter Nine

Power in Weakness

Are they Hebrews? So am I. Are they Israelites? So am I. Are they descendants of Abraham? So am I. Are they ministers of Christ? I am talking like a madman—I am a better one: with far greater labors, far more imprisonments, with countless floggings, and often near death. Five times I have received from the Jews the forty lashes minus one. Three times I was beaten with rods. Once I received a stoning. Three times I was shipwrecked; for a night and a day I was adrift at sea; on frequent journeys, in danger from rivers, danger from bandits, danger from my own people, danger from Gentiles, danger in the city, danger in the wilderness, danger at sea, danger from false brothers and sisters; in toil and hardship, through many a sleepless night, hungry and thirsty, often without food, cold and naked. (2 Corinthians 11:22-27)

Happy Valley Community Church was outgrowing its current building so they decided to expand and buy land and build a large sanctuary. They saved money, bought a nice piece of property, and hired a local architect. They were excited. A few months went by and the architect told them he was finished with the renderings. He met with the building committee. They were thrilled. The Church was nestled on the side of a hill and they used granite from a nearby quarry. A cloister walk connected the Church building with the hall. The inside was quite beautiful too; large hand hewn oak timbers stained dark brown and flagstone flooring and stained glass windows.

One evening during a building committee meeting, some folks requested a short break so that they could deliberate. The architect got up and went into the kitchen for some snacks and coffee. After a while they called him back and said, "You know, we love the building. We love the cloister walk, it combines both the old world and the new world, and the bell tower is gorgeous too. But we want you to make a small change if you don't mind." He said, "Sure, no problem, anything is fine." They said, "There's too many crosses. We want you to remove them." The architect thought they were crazy, "But you're a Church," he said. "Oh yes," they said, "we are, but we don't want people to focus so much on death. We want people to focus on *Happy* and *Community,* leave them with good feelings."

My power is made perfect in weakness.

We live in a world that praises power and authority, heroism and strength. We learn to climb the corporate ladder. We're taught to outwit everyone else and make sure we get the prize.

In the ancient world there was a man named Daedalus. Daedalus was a famous artist. He was a potter and a jeweler and made beautiful things out of silver and gold. He had a son named Icarus. King Minos, a famous king from Crete, wanted Daedalus to build a labyrinth in his garden. So Daedalus traveled to Crete with Icarus and they constructed a huge labyrinth. It was the best labyrinth in the land.

Chapter Nine

When it was time for Daedalus and Icarus to leave the King said, "No. You must stay. I want you to build other things for me." But Daedalus had a wife and a family back home. He wanted to leave so he and Icarus walked to the harbor and the king had guards at the harbor so they couldn't take a ship home. One day Daedalus looked up and saw hawks and eagles flying high above and said, "We can fly home." Icarus collected some bird feathers and Daedalus collected some wood and wax and they began their project. Daedalus softened the wax and put the bird feathers in the wax. They attached the feathers to the wood.

Then, on a windy day, they went to the highest mountain on Crete, they could see the entire sea and the fish and the dolphins below so they ran and jumped and they started flying and they kept flapping their wings. Daedalus looked back and saw Icarus flying up towards the sky and called out, "No Icarus, you cannot fly up there, the sun's too hot." Icarus said, "I want to see the sun and the stars and the moon." But Icarus kept flying towards the sun, the closer he got the wax melted, the feathers fell out, and he fell down and sank right into the ocean. My mom would have said that Icarus was too big for his britches. He was too full of himself. He wanted to do things his way rather than his father's way. He was headstrong and wouldn't listen. If he did listen he'd be home safe with his father.

My power is made perfect in weakness.

There was a pastor who had been in a parish for a few months and a member of the parish council, a business man and leader, approached him after Sunday services and said, "Pastor, you know, I'd like to help you. I've been in business a few years and when I started my company I had three employees and ten thousand dollars. Now I have thirty employees and three million dollars. I'd like to take you out to lunch and make a few suggestions on how you can improve your leadership skills." The pastor agreed and they met for lunch. Midway through lunch the man said, "You know pastor, I really like your preaching but I noticed that about every five weeks you talk about suffering, maybe you can stop talking about suffering so much?" So the pastor said fine. Then the man continued, "You know," he said, "You also talk about being weak too much. Not good. People are weak as it is. They are vulnerable and broken. They know that. Talk about something nice, something that will improve their spirits. Make them laugh a little, be happy. And there's just one more thing I want to tell you. I noticed that you always talk about the cross way too much. That's a no, no. The cross is a downer, it reminds folks about death." The pastor said, "But isn't the cross the center of our faith?" "Oh sure," the businessman said, "But you know, Easter is more than the cross, it's about the flowers and the springtime. Jesus also talked a lot about the flowers of the field and the birds of the air. Maybe focus more on flowers and such rather than the cross." The pastor went home dejected and depressed.

My power is made perfect in weakness.

Paul reminds us that God's ways are not our ways. We live in a world where we value strength and hero worship.

We value power and profit. We don't value weakness and smallness. We live in a world that is upwardly mobile.

Jesus' way is downward mobility. Jesus shows us that we are supposed to get down, actually get down on our knees and wash peoples' feet, get down and dirty in the grit and the grime of life. According to the gospel the cross is a symbol of shame and humility, of death and destruction. But for us, those who believe and follow Jesus, the cross is a sign of power, strength, and love.

My power is made perfect in weakness.

Yes, we are weak. Yes we are limited. Yes we are vulnerable. Yet we are not alone. Jesus is with us in his weakness because his power is made perfect in weakness, and so is ours.

Food For Thought

1. The world doesn't honor weakness, but God does. We want to shrug off our weakness and highlight our strength. We know that God's ways are different. When we embrace our weakness we are on the road to healing and wholeness. Take some time and think about your weakness and how God might use this for your salvation.

2. The cross is the center of our life. Take some time and meditate on the cross, on Jesus's sacrifice for us. How can you better embrace the

cross in your life? How can you embrace Jesus' sacrifice in your family and in your parish?

3. Read: Psalm 34:17-20, 2 Corinthians 12:9, Romans 12:9

Chapter Ten

The Land of Zebulun and Naphtali

Now when Jesus heard that John had been arrested, he withdrew to Galilee. He left Nazareth and made his home in Capernaum by the sea, in the territory of Zebulun and Naphtali, so that what had been spoken through the prophet Isaiah might be fulfilled: "Land of Zebulun, land of Naphtali, on the road by the sea, across the Jordan, Galilee of the Gentiles— the people who sat in darkness have seen a great light, and for those who sat in the region and shadow of death light has dawned." From that time Jesus began to proclaim, "Repent, for the kingdom of heaven has come near." (Matthew 4:12-17)

Near the beginning of Matthew we hear a passage from Isaiah, "The land of Zebulun and the land of Naphtali, across the sea, towards the Jordan, the Galilee of the Gentiles, the people who have sat in darkness."

Reading the Old Testament we know that Israel was divided into twelve tribes and each tribe was allotted a parcel of land. Zebulun and Naphtali were situated between the Jordan River to the East and the Mediterranean Sea on the West. This area is fertile farmland Zebulun and the land of Naphtali were the breadbasket of Israel; they grew wheat, bananas, figs, dates, almonds, oranges, thyme, basil, and onions. Zebulun and Naphtali were located along a trading route that went from Turkey in the north all the way to Egypt in the southwest. Caravans traveled through the area and traded gold, silver, and silk for food. Zebulun and

Naphtali were rich. They were living in the land of milk and honey, of riches and bounties.

There was an Assyrian ruler in the north, Tiglath-Pileser who wanted the figs and oranges and dates and almonds, but he didn't want to trade his gold, or silver or silk. No. He wanted it all for himself. He took his armies and his chariots and his men and invaded Zebulun and Naphtali. He pillaged the villages and wreaked havoc for the farms. The people who lived in the land of milk and honey, the people of the Promised Land, were now living in darkness and despair.

Isaiah continues and says that God allowed Tiglath-Pileser to invade Zebulun and Naphtali. Allowed? Yes, allowed. I know it sounds strange but it's true. Why? Because the Israelites turned away from him. The people in Zebulun and Naphtali brought the darkness upon themselves. They took their gold and silver and melted it and made idols and false gods where they worshipped on the mountaintops. They were in darkness because they loved these false idols and not the one true God, the God of Abraham, Isaac, and Jacob. They were in darkness because they no longer helped the widow and the orphan. They were in darkness because they worshipped false gods.

Even though we live in a much different world than Isaiah did, we are just like the people in Zebulun and Naphtali. We are in darkness when we turn away from God. We are in darkness when we replace God with false idols. We are in darkness when we cause fights and friction in our family. We are in darkness when we lie or judge or make fun of people because of their religion and race.

Like many boys my age, I had a paper route in Middle School. I delivered newspapers to sixty homes in a five-block area. The papers would be delivered to my doorstep in a shrink-wrapped cube which the truck driver would put on our doorstep. I'd get up before sunrise, put the papers in my grocery cart, and deliver them to the customers. I did this seven days a week; winter, spring, summer, and fall. I paid a friend to deliver the papers when our family went on vacation.

Sometimes I got tired of delivering the papers. One early spring day I wanted to sleep in. When I heard the paper truck coming I quickly ran downstairs. Mom and dad were still sleeping. I took the shrink-wrapped cube and put it behind the garage. I thought no one would find them there. I returned back inside and fell asleep.

Later that morning Mom was in the kitchen making toast and eggs and asked, "How was the paper route?" "Fine," I said. "Oh, that's good," she said. After eating breakfast dad came in and said, "I need some help." And I said, "Oh, what kind of help do you want?" "Oh, not much just some yard work. I'm spreading mulch today." He said. "Ah, maybe I will help mom do the laundry." I said. "No." he said, "I really need your help. Don't dilly dally either."

I walked outside and followed dad behind the garage. He pointed to the cube of papers sitting on top of the mulch pile, "You go inside and apologize to Mom for lying. Then you deliver all of those papers and apologize to each one of those customers for being late and don't you ever do this again!" I was in darkness. I lied to both my mom and disrespected my customers for not delivering their papers on time. Years later I wondered what would have happened if dad didn't make me apologize to mom. You know how life can be, one thing easily leads to another; lying can lead to cheating, cheating can lead to stealing, and stealing, stealing can lead to drugs, and drugs can lead to, well, a lot of bad things. Perhaps if dad never made me apologize I would be in prison and not a pastor.

Isaiah doesn't end with darkness. The passage continues, "The people who sat in darkness, *have seen a great light.*" Isaiah knew that even though the people of Zebulun and Naphtali were in darkness that one day God would save them. That no matter how far they turned from God that God was always there for them and that he would lead them into the light.

Jesus Christ is our light. He is our light that shows us the way back to God. Every time we love God we are in the light. Every time we help those in need we are in the light. Every time we put God in the center of our life we are in the light. Every time we are honest and truthful we are in the light. Every time we follow God's commandments we are in the light. Let's keep walking in the light and share this light with others, God knows the world needs it.

Food For Thought

1. Was there ever a time when you felt like you were in darkness? What was the specific situation? How did you get out of the darkness?

2. Most of the time we are blind to the fact that we are in darkness. I am grateful for my father for leading me to the light. Hopefully someone in our life, our spouse, our children, even a friend will confront us with our darkness and lead us to the light.

3. Read: Matthew 5:16, John 9:1-10, Isaiah 60:1-10

Chapter Eleven

On the Jericho Road

"He entered Jericho and was passing through it. A man was there named Zacchaeus; he was a chief tax collector and was rich. He was trying to see who Jesus was, but on account of the crowd he could not, because he was short in stature. So he ran ahead and climbed a sycamore tree to see him, because he was going to pass that way. When Jesus came to the place, he looked up and said to him, "Zacchaeus, hurry and come down; for I must stay at your house today." So he hurried down and was happy to welcome him. All who saw it began to grumble and said, "He has gone to be the guest of one who is a sinner." Zacchaeus stood there and said to the Lord, "Look, half of my possessions, Lord, I will give to the poor; and if I have defrauded anyone of anything, I will pay back four times as much." Then Jesus said to him, "Today salvation has come to this house, because he too is a son of Abraham. For the Son of Man came to seek out and to save the lost." (Luke 19:1-10)

According to the gospels Jesus lived in Nazareth. Nazareth is located in the northern part of the Galilee in a fertile plain. Traveling further south the terrain is less green, less fertile, and less shady. You enter into hot, dry, dusty areas. There is little water. There are hills and mountains and crags and caves. After a while you reach the Judean desert and the Dead Sea which is literally a liquid desert. Scientists say that the ocean is around three percent salt and the Dead Sea is around thirty four percent; you don't swim in the Dead Sea, you float.

Jericho is on the edge of the Dead Sea and its mentioned very early in the Bible.

Joshua led the Israelites into the Promised Land. But before they entered the Promised Land they had to conquer Jericho. But the men of Jericho had swords and slingshots and catapults and clearly outnumbered the Israelites. Joshua said, "Lord, you lead us out of Egypt, you lead us through the Red Sea, you lead us through the desert, and now you are leading us to our destruction?" The Lord always has a plan. The Lord told Joshua don't worry. He instructed them to take the Ark of the Covenant which contained the Ten Commandments, and seven priests, and march around the city once every day for six days. On the seventh day they were to march around the city seven times and after the seventh time they were to blow their horns and the walls would come tumbling down. So the Israelites did that. For six days they marched around the city one time and on the seventh day they blew their horns and the walls came tumbling down. Joshua and his men conquered Jericho and entered into the Promised Land.

Luke tells us that when Jesus entered Jericho he met a chief tax collector named Zacchaeus, "Zacchaeus, come down now for I am going to your house today." Zacchaeus said that he would give half of his goods to the poor and if he defrauded anyone he would restore it fourfold. Jesus doesn't accuse Zacchaeus of anything, he doesn't make him feel guilty or get angry with him he just says that he's coming over his house. When Zacchaeus encountered Jesus the walls came tumbling down; the walls between

Zacchaeus and Jesus; the walls between Zacchaeus and his fellow Jews. Then Jesus says, "Today salvation has come to his house for he also is a son of Abraham" (Luke 19:9).

Humans like building walls. The Great Wall of China was built to keep out the Mongolians. The wall around Gaza and the West bank was built to keep the Palestinians out of Israel. The wall in Cyprus, which is actually a tall fence with chicken wire, divides the Turkish controlled north and the Greek controlled area in the south. Then there are the invisible walls that we put up around us; the invisible walls of apartheid in South Africa and the invisible walls in the United States that kept the Native Americans on reservations, separated from everyone else.

In 1987 former President Ronald Reagan stood in front of the Brandenburg Gate in Berlin. The Brandenburg Gate divided East and West Germany. It was a wall of power, a wall of control, a wall of that separated families and friends. In his now famous speech President Regan said, "Premier Gorbachev, tear down this wall." It took two years, but finally that wall came tumbling down.

It's hard to be vulnerable, to put yourself out there every day. It hurts when you love others and they don't love you back. It hurts when you love others and they don't love you at all. It hurts when people reject you. Yet love is the Christian way. Love is the way of Jesus. Hopefully the walls that we make for ourselves, the walls between husbands and wives, between parents and children, between our neighbors, come tumbling down. For today salvation has come to our house.

Food for Thought

1. Take some time and think about all the walls and barriers that separate you from someone or something else. Walls are usually built out of fear. What are you afraid of? Take some time and meditate on the physical, spiritual, and emotional walls that you have. Are there ways to slowly tear down the walls?

2. When we erect walls we prevent communication and love from flowing freely.

3. Read: 1 Samuel 18:10-11, 2 Chronicles 14:7, Joshua 2:15

Chapter Twelve

Life is Complicated

He put before them another parable: "The kingdom of heaven may be compared to someone who sowed good seed in his field; but while everybody was asleep, an enemy came and sowed weeds among the wheat, and then went away. So when the plants came up and bore grain, then the weeds appeared as well. And the slaves of the householder came and said to him, 'Master, did you not sow good seed in your field? Where, then, did these weeds come from?' He answered, 'An enemy has done this.' The slaves said to him, 'Then do you want us to go and gather them?' But he replied, 'No; for in gathering the weeds you would uproot the wheat along with them. Let both of them grow together until the harvest; and at harvest time I will tell the reapers, Collect the weeds first and bind them in bundles to be burned, but gather the wheat into my barn.'" (Matthew 13:24-30)

The other day I was cleaning out my office closet. Most folks have a junk drawer, I have a junk closet. Over the years I have thrown everything in there, old papers, cancelled checks, recipes, pictures, college and seminary notes. Every time we moved I pushed a lot of stuff into the closet. The other day I was frustrated because I couldn't see the floor anymore, a sign that I needed to do something. I thought it was going to be an easy project, over and done with. I was wrong.

I thought I'd have two piles: one pile for keeping and the other pile for the garbage. After a while I realized it wasn't so easy. At the end of the day I had four piles. The "things to keep pile" was the smallest followed by "to be shredded pile" which was the slightly bigger. The "recycling pile" was even bigger, and the "not sure pile" was the biggest pile of them all. I came across photos and pictures thinking that maybe one day my children or grandchildren would want them.

By Wednesday I recycled the papers in the recycling pile, shredded the stuff in the shredding pile, and some of the things in the not sure about pile? Well, I still wasn't sure about them so I packed them up and put them neatly in the closet. Maybe five years from now I'll go through the box again. For now I'm done. At least I can see the closet floor.

As I was going through the piles I thought how easy life was when I was a kid, everything was black and white, good and bad. There wasn't much grey.

In the summer we played good cop and bad cop. I liked to be the bad cop with my cap guns, shooting everyone and pretending to rob banks and hiding behind trees. We played cowboys and Indians, cowboys were good and Indians were bad. We also played a game called Mafia, I'm not sure what that was about it must have been pretty clear to me back then. As I got older I realized that most of life is not always black and white nor is it easy. Life is pretty darn difficult at times.

Every day we commemorate a different saint on the Church calendar: Saint John the Baptist, Saint Mary Magdalene, Saint Peter, Saint Andrew, Saint Paul, and others. Among the saints in the Orthodox Church that we celebrate is Saint Vladimir, Enlightener of Russia and Equal to the Apostles. There are many different types of saints: missionary saints, soldier saints, priest saints, monastic saints, miracle working saints, but very few that are called Equal to the Apostles. That title is reserved just for a few like Saint Vladimir.

The popular story about Saint Vladimir reports that he wanted to have power over all the Rus' tribes. There were dozens of these small tribes of peasants and warriors but they were disorganized. Vladimir wanted a common faith tradition which would unite all of these tribes and make him a very powerful prince. Some tribes worshipped the sun, some worshipped the stars, and others worshipped Mother Earth. But Vladimir wanted something bigger, something greater than that so he sent envoys to Jerusalem to check out the Jewish people, he sent envoys to Mecca and Medina to check out the Muslims, and finally he sent envoys to check out the Orthodox Christians in Constantinople. After a while all the envoys returned and they reported what they experienced.

The envoys from Constantinople returned and were so excited, they said that they didn't know whether they were in earth or heaven. They reported that the music, icons, incense, and vestments were so beautiful that they were overwhelming. After hearing all of that, Vladimir decided to have all the Rus' tribes baptized. He told the tribes that they can all jump in the river. However, this wasn't much of a choice since behind them on the shore were soldiers armed with swords and clubs to prevent anyone from escaping. Yet despite Vladimir's less than honorable attitude he is still remembered in the Church as the Enlightener of Russia and Equal to the Apostles.

Every Sunday I stand in front of the altar table wearing my beautiful vestments offering our common praise and prayer over the gifts of bread and wine. I preach a sermon and teach the faith. I talk with folks during coffee hour. Yet I have said some things that I'm embarrassed about, done things that I'm ashamed of, and had thoughts that I'm both ashamed and embarrassed of. Yet despite all of that, I still stand in front of the altar each Sunday in my beautiful vestments offering thanksgiving over bread and wine, preach a sermon, teach the faith, and talk with folks at coffee hour. Life isn't always so clear is it?

In the parable of the wheat and the weeds there is a rich man who has a big farm and his servants plant wheat. After planting the fields they wake up one morning and see that there are weeds growing, not small ones but big weeds, weeds that will take over the wheat. Weeds that will soak up all the rain, take all the nutrients and fertilizer from the ground, and use up the sun's rays. The servants are mad and they tell their master all of this and he says, "No worries, just let the wheat and the weeds grow up together and at the harvest we'll take care of it." The servants are still angry about the weeds and they remind the master about the weeds and he tells them that they should let the wheat and weeds grow up together and in the end he will decide which is the wheat and which are the weeds, but until then they must let things just be as they are.

It's not up for us to judge others. It's not up to us even to judge ourselves. All we can do is be faithful in the small daily tasks of life and let the chips fall where they may. Only God is the judge and we put our faith in the fact that as a judge our Lord is caring and compassionate.

Food For Thought

1. Jesus warns us not to judge others. It's hard but we shouldn't judge other people. Things may look clear from our perspective but there's a big chance that we don't see things clearly. Life is often more complicated and complex than we think.

2. Take some time to read through the parable of the wheat and the weeds (Matthew 13:24-30). What do you find difficult in the parable? What do you find consoling? What do you find disturbing? Read this same parable again the following week. Do you see anything new or interesting in it?

3. Read: Matthew 7:1-5, James 4:11-12, Luke 6:37

Chapter Thirteen

Faithful Not Fickle

The next day the great crowd that had come to the festival heard that Jesus was coming to Jerusalem. So they took branches of palm trees and went out to meet him, shouting, "Hosanna! Blessed is the one who comes in the name of the Lord— the King of Israel!" Jesus found a young donkey and sat on it; as it is written: "Do not be afraid, daughter of Zion. Look, your king is coming, sitting on a donkey's colt!" (John 12:12-16)

In early spring many states hold local elections. The candidates put their slick slogans on bumper stickers, posters, and placards anywhere and everywhere. Politicians look good in their dapper suits and well coiffed hair. We hear stump speeches and watch compelling television advertisements. We hear promises about more jobs, greater economic prosperity, and lower taxes. And what do we do? We vote for them. A few months go by and then when taxes aren't lower and the economy is still bad and there are few new jobs what do we do? We vote them out of office.

We're more fickle than faithful.

Christians are fickle too. There was a pastor who was retiring after serving the parish for many years. The parish wanted a younger more energetic pastor, someone with a family. After a long search they finally found one. The new pastor was young and intelligent, a Harvard Seminary graduate, married, and had a lovely wife and two young children. They were a perfect family. He did all the right things too; he preached, he visited folks, and he was active in the local community.

A few months went by. After Sunday worship, folks gathered like they usually do in the parking lot and engaged in a traditional Christian pastime of Church gossip. One person said, "Oh, the pastor is so nice and all but you know, his sermons, they're too long. Our former pastor's sermons were five or ten minutes. This guy goes on for fifteen, twenty, even thirty-five minutes sometimes." Another person said, "Yeah, that's not all. Did you notice that his wife is hardly in Church? Sure, she sings in the choir and all but our old pastor's wife, boy she was involved with Church school, with the flower committee, and with the beautification committee." Someone else piped up, "Yeah, and those children! Sure they're cute, but they're hellions, running all over the place and wreaking havoc on Sunday. Our older pastor, boy, his kids were well behaved." A few months later the pastor was asked to leave.

The parish council wanted to show leadership and that they were forward thinking and creative so they chose a female pastor to replace him. They found a wonderful pastor who was married but didn't have children. This didn't bother most parishioners because they thought they'd have children later.

Just like the previous pastor, this one was nice. She preached sermons, she visited parishioners, she baptized babies, and married couples. Then one Sunday after services a few parishioners were chatting in the parking lot, "Our new pastor is fine and all, but have you noticed that her sermons are short? She just gets going and then she stops, it's like I leave Church half empty half the time." And other parishioner piped up, "Yeah, and her husband. Have you noticed that he is involved in everything? I mean really. He's on the building committee, he's on the parish council, he's on the Education task force, he's everywhere!" And then another person piped up, "Yeah, and they don't have any children yet, when is she going to get pregnant?" Someone responded, "Well you know what I heard? I heard that they don't even want to have children." Someone else overheard that and said, "What, no children! We want our pastor to have children." So guess what happened. A few months later, just like the previous pastor, this one was gone too.

We're more fickle than faithful.

Even though you might not agree with me, even though you might think I'm dead wrong, it's true; we are a fickle bunch. One day we're hot the next day we're cold. Don't worry, we're not alone either, they're plenty of fickle people in Scripture.

Isaiah, Jeremiah, Ezekiel, Amos, Hosea, all talk about a savior who will come and save the Israelites. They talk about the coming Kingdom of God. They all talk about someone who will bring justice and order. The messiah finally came. His name was Jesus. But people expected someone else. They expected someone who would fight the Romans. They expected someone who would bring economic prosperity. They expected someone who would lower taxes and bring a better government. Jesus didn't meet their expectations because he didn't come with soldiers and an army, he didn't overthrow the Roman rule, and he didn't bring a new world order. He did none of that. No. He came humbly on a donkey. He came by himself with no armies or soldiers. He came to take his throne which was the cross.

On that first Palm Sunday in Jerusalem all the people came out holding their palms in their hands and shouting, "Hosanna, Hosanna, blessed is he who comes in the name of the Lord." Six days later shouted, "Crucify Him, Crucify Him." The crowd that came out and was thrilled that Jesus was coming; six days later raised their arms and shouted, "Let his blood be on us and on our children." The same crowd who came out by the thousands on that first Palm Sunday later abandoned him six days later. Matthew, Luke, and John say that a few people were there at the foot of the cross. Mark reminds us that Jesus died alone between two thieves.

So much for our faithfulness.

Yet we still say, "If I were there I'd be different. I'd follow him all the way to the end and I'd stay by is side even at the cross." Yeah, right. Even two-thousand years after Jesus we are still more fickle than faithful. My hunch is that if Jesus were still here today we'd just be as fickle at those crowds in Jerusalem.

Despite the fact that we often lack faith and hope, the fact that we are often hard hearted and self centered and jealous and angry. Despite the fact that we often abandon him, Jesus still comes to us, on his donkey, as our messiah, our savior, and still goes to his throne, the cross. He does this because while we are fickle most of the time, he is not. God is always faithful.

Food For Thought

1. Have there been key moments in life when you had a weak faith? Take some time and write down the circumstances of each event. If these events happened now would you act differently or the same? Why or why not?

2. I find it comforting that many people in the Bible had times of doubt; Saint Thomas, Saint Paul, and Saint Joseph come to mind. Do you identify with anyone in the Scriptures that had a weak faith?

3. Read: Proverbs 3:5-8, Matthew 21:21, Romans 10:17

Chapter Fourteen

Back to School Blues

"As he was setting out on a journey, a man ran up and knelt before him, and asked him, "Good Teacher, what must I do to inherit eternal life?" Jesus said to him, "Why do you call me good? No one is good but God alone. You know the commandments: 'You shall not murder; You shall not commit adultery; You shall not steal; You shall not bear false witness; You shall not defraud; Honor your father and mother.'" He said to him, "Teacher, I have kept all these since my youth." Jesus, looking at him, loved him and said, "You lack one thing; go, sell what you own, and give the money to the poor, and you will have treasure in heaven; then come, follow me." When he heard this, he was shocked and went away grieving, for he had many possessions." (Mark 10:17-31)

It's back to school time and back to school means new books backpacks, packing snacks and lunches, waking up early, carpooling, and waiting for the bus.

Back to school also means quizzes, exams, and papers. I remember sitting in high school and college classes and asking the teacher what I have to do to get an A in the class. He or she would say, come to all the classes, do all the readings, and write perfect papers and you'll get an A. Then I asked well, what about a B? So they said do so-so on the papers, you can miss a few classes, and you can do so-so on the quizzes. I wasn't dumb enough to ask about a C. In my family a C was average and my parents didn't want average, they wanted above average so I always wanted to strive for the best.

Back to school also means school plays, band, and sports. Every year our school had a play, usually one in the fall and then one in the spring. If you wanted to try out for the play you had to prepare to recite a few lines, and then be willing to come to all the play practices, dress rehearsals, and the performances. If it was a musical you also had to prepare a song to sing or prepare a short dance routine. I said no way was I going to do all of that. I'd much rather be one of those behind the scene guys and help paint props.

The situation pertains with sports teams. If you want to make the soccer team you have to get a physical, you have to get a concussion test, you have to spend two or three days doing tryouts and then if you are really, really good, you'll make the team.

What both of these scenarios have in common is that they both rely on me: what do I have to do to get an A on this quiz, what do I have to do to get an A in the class, what do I have to do to get on the soccer team or in the school musical. What's in my power and how can I accomplish it. We think that somehow we have the authority, power, and talent which helps us get ahead in life.

The rich man in the gospel reading clearly wants to get ahead. He comes to Jesus asking what must he do to inherit eternal life, as if he has any power to do anything. But surely you've met folks like him, people who have power and prestige, people who have money and material possessions who assume that they can throw their weight around just because they are rich and because everyone else looks up to them. As the old saying goes: money makes the world go around.

But this isn't how Jesus works. Just because the rich man is wealthy he assumes that he can push Jesus around. Jesus doesn't budge one bit, he tells the rich man that if you want to be perfect, go get rid of what you have and then follow me. Matthew gives us a one line zinger too; the guy went away sad because he had too many riches. He went away sorrowful because he couldn't use his power or influence or money to get what he wanted. Jesus packs a punch.

Jesus tells the rich man that if you want to be a part of me and my friends you have to divest yourself of all the things that are controlling you. You have to lessen your load and follow. Yet we still think, because we are a part of this world, that Jesus is wrong and we are right. We can keep hitting our head on the wall, but Jesus isn't going to budge. He tells us, as he told the rich man, "Go, sell your possessions, and come follow me." Are you up for the challenge?

Food For Thought

1. Jesus is direct with the rich man. Jesus commands him to sell all that he has, share it with the poor, and follow Jesus. The man goes away sad because he has too many possessions. Jesus is direct with us too. We have more than enough material items than we need and probably enough for two lifetimes.

2. Being one of Jesus' disciples means that we have to leave certain things behind in order to follow his teaching. Take a few moments and look at your life. What are the material, physical, or spiritual things which prevent you from following Jesus? Keep this list handy and reflect on it from time to time to see if you have made progress on it.

3. Read: John 8:12, Acts 2:21, 1 Corinthians 11:1

Chapter Fifteen

Imitate Me

For I think that God has exhibited us apostles as last of all, as though sentenced to death, because we have become a spectacle to the world, to angels and to mortals. We are fools for the sake of Christ, but you are wise in Christ. We are weak, but you are strong. You are held in honor, but we in disrepute. To the present hour we are hungry and thirsty, we are poorly clothed and beaten and homeless, and we grow weary from the work of our own hands. When reviled, we bless; when persecuted, we endure; when slandered, we speak kindly. We have become like the rubbish of the world, the dregs of all things, to this very day. I am not writing this to make you ashamed, but to admonish you as my beloved children. For though you might have ten thousand guardians in Christ, you do not have many fathers. Indeed, in Christ Jesus I became your father through the gospel. I appeal to you, then, be imitators of me. (1 Corinthians 4:16-23)

I love watching little children, especially babies and toddlers. They are so cute and cuddly. They can't communicate much but they will mimic you. If you put your hands over your eyes and say "peek-a-boo" they will say "peek-a-boo" back. If you stand in place and stomp your feet they'll stomp their feet too. Whatever you do they will do too.

Ask any educator and they'll basically tell you the same thing. Children learn by doing as much as they do by hearing. The animal kingdom is no different. If a momma bear sees her baby cub heading near a fast moving river or stream she'll most likely walk over, pick up the bear cub by the scruff of his neck, and bring him to higher ground. Now if the cub is smart the momma bear will only have to do that once. If not it may take a few more tries. After two or three times doing this the little bear cub should get the hint; river bad, momma good. I guarantee you that when that bear cub becomes a momma or daddy bear cub he or she will do the same thing with their cubs. Learning by watching.

Paul is speaking to the Corinthian Church and from what read in the Book of Acts he spent a year and a half in Corinth. He ate with them, he met with them, he worshipped with them, and he laughed and cried with them. Now some time passes and he finds out that there's all sorts of trouble brewing in Corinth, jealousy, pride, and envy. Paul tells them look at my life, look what I did, if you want to be a part of this new thing called the Christian community you need get your act together. You need to begin acting like Christians and not like little babies anymore. He says this not to make them feel bad, not to make him look good, but to make them realize that his life is an example for them. He ends this passage with the words, "imitate me." Do what I did. Paul's life and legacy is an example for the Corinthians. People may not have remembered exactly what he told them but they can certainly remember his actions.

I had a lot of teachers in my life: Church school teachers, middle school and high school teachers, college and seminary teachers. However the one teacher whom I remember the most is Mrs. Vivorito.

Mrs. Vivorito was my fifth grade Church School teacher. I don't remember anything she said, but I do remember her. She always brought her older daughter to services with her and both of them stood on the other side of the Church. She was kind and that I always saw her put an envelope in the collection basket. She sticks in my mind as someone very important, yet I don't recall a word she said. That's the power of example.

Our lives can be great examples to others. Both children and adults learn from our actions, we behave and how we act. Recently a Catholic bishop from Central America said that we need to be careful of our actions because we might be the only witness to the gospel that someone will encounter in their lives. We tend to forget how important our actions really are, the way we carry ourselves and the way that we treat others. As Paul says, imitate me because when you imitate me you are doing what Christ did.

Food For Thought

1. There is a common saying that says: actions speak louder than words. People take note of our actions and how we conduct our daily affairs. How do you conduct your life? If a stranger meets you will they see you as loving, kind, and grateful? Will they know that you are a follower of Jesus?

2. Does your life imitate the life of Paul or Jesus? Do you strive to live in a godly manner? If not, you can always start.

3. Read: Deuteronomy 32:2, James 3:1-2, Titus 2:7-8

Chapter Sixteen

You Can Do It

"A week later his disciples were again in the house, and Thomas was with them. Although the doors were shut, Jesus came and stood among them and said, "Peace be with you." Then he said to Thomas, "Put your finger here and see my hands. Reach out your hand and put it in my side. Do not doubt but believe." Thomas answered him, "My Lord and my God!" Jesus said to him, "Have you believed because you have seen me? Blessed are those who have not seen and yet have come to believe." Now Jesus did many other signs in the presence of his disciples, which are not written in this book. But these are written so that you may come to believe that Jesus is the Messiah, the Son of God, and that through believing you may have life in his name." (John 20:26-30)

When reading Scripture it's easy to miss important details. I do it all the time. It's like taking a walk through a park and seeing a bird but not knowing what type of bird it is. I can tell the difference between a Robin and a Cardinal, between a Bluebird and a Blue Jay, but that's about it. Once we went bird watching underneath a tall canopy of trees. The guide said he knew that there were Bluebirds and Hawks around, yet I didn't see any birds. He located the birds by hearing not by sight. Toward the end of the walk he told us that he heard a hawk high above us in one of the trees, and I said, "Yeah, right!" He popped open his telescope on his traveling tripod and invited me to look through the lens. He was right. It was a big beautiful red tailed Hawk.

The Bible is no different than my walk in the woods. It's common that most folks read the passage from John and immediately focus on Thomas. We often use the phrase "he's a doubting Thomas" for people who doubt and have little faith. Most folks focus on Thomas but overlook the beginning of the passage.

John says that the first Sunday after Easter the apostles were still in the upper room in Jerusalem. They were scared because they saw their friend arrested. They were scared because they saw their friend put on trial and beaten and crucified. They were anxious because they had no leader. They were fearful because they had no plan, no direction, and no guidance. For three years Jesus was with them and now he wasn't. Yet the week after Easter the risen Lord comes through the closed doors and three times says, "Peace be with you." He then breathes on them and says, "As the Father has sent me, so too, I send you." Another way of putting that is, "You can do it." You can continue my preaching and teaching ministry. You can continue spreading the good news. You can continue your walk of faith. In other words: you can do it.

There once was a young high school couple that was madly in love. They were both eighteen and were married soon after graduation. They wanted to go to college. They wanted good jobs. They wanted to buy a house. They wanted the American dream. Soon afterwards they were married the girl was pregnant with twins. The husband thought that if he signed up for the army and stayed in four years he could then retire and then go to college. The extra pay would help with the children and the household expenses. So he enrolled in the Army. It was August 2001.

September 11 was around the corner. The United States invaded Iraq. His battalion was called up. He eventually died in battle. His wife was home alone. She wanted to terminate the pregnancy. When she went home to tell her plan to her parents her mom responded, "No. You can do this. You can have the baby." She said, "But mom what about college?" Her mom replied, "I can watch the baby three mornings a week and dad can watch them twice a week and grandma is around so she can help too." "But mom," She said, "what about work? Her mom said, "You can do this. You can work part time a few hours a week at the library and save up some money." She said, "But mom…' and her mom said, "no but's, you can do this." And she did.

When I graduated from seminary I didn't have a job right away. I wasn't ready to take a parish yet and there's not much you can do with a theology degree other than serve as a pastor. I was job hunting and there were no leads. I tried teaching jobs but there was nothing. Finally when I was at wits end, the Dean of students asked me to see him in his office. He told me that he heard that I was looking for work and was wondering if I found anything. I told him that I didn't have a job yet. He then said the he had a job for me, "Oh, is it painting? I've done some painting before," I asked. He said, "No." I said, "Is it landscaping? I've done some landscaping before." He said "No." I then said, "Okay, what is it?" He said that they needed a cook. I said, "Absolutely not." He said, "You can do this."

The job included cooking for fifty men, two meals a day. I had cooked for my wife and maybe a few friends, but that was it. He said you can do it. He told me to talk with the kitchen manager and see what she said. So I did. I walked down the hallway and told the kitchen manager all what we talked about and she said, "You can do this." I said, "Maybe you can do this but not me." She said, "I'll help you. I'll help you make a month of menus and go shopping with you and show you the ropes. She said go talk to the business manager at the seminary and see what he says. So I did. I told him everything that the Dean of students told me and the business manager and he said, "You can do this." I said, "Maybe you can do this but I can't." He said, "Yes you can." And I did. For three years I cooked two meals a day for five days a week. Even now I can't believe how I did that.

On that first Easter the Risen Lord came into the upper room and told the disciples, "As the Father has sent me, so too I send you" (John 19:17). The Risen Lord sent the disciples into the world to continue his preaching and teaching ministry. He sent them into the world to continue the walk of faith. He sent them into the world to share the good news. He told them, yes you might be afraid, yes you might have doubts, yes you may have anxiety, but you can do this.

The Risen Lord comes to us today and tells us, "You can do it." I'm sure many of us have heavy hearts even after the Easter has come and gone. We might have fears about our future, fears about our marriages, fears about our finances, fears about what to do in life. Yet the Risen Lord reminds us, just as the Father has sent me, so too I send you. You can do this. I hope we can all answer, "Yes we can!"

Food For Thought

1. There are days when I feel like I have a strong faith but there are more times when I feel like Thomas. There are days when I am filled with doubt and despair. It's okay to have doubts about our faith. It's natural. Do you have times of great doubt?

2. When I look at some of the big saints of the Church, Saint Nicholas, Saint Herman of Alaska, Saint Raphael of Brooklyn, and others I wonder how did they accomplish such great things? How did they do what they did? The answer is that they did small things all the time that were little bits of light, love, and joy. Every time they showed light, love, and joy they made the world a better place. While we cannot end poverty, homelessness, or hunger, we can certainly help alleviate some suffering around us. Take some time and reflect on the phrase "Yes you can." What can you do in your little life that will create more light, love, and joy?

3. Read: Psalm 23:1-6, 1 Thessalonians 5:11, Hebrews 3:13

Chapter Seventeen

Come and See

Philip found Nathanael and said to him, "We have found him about whom Moses in the law and also the prophets wrote, Jesus son of Joseph from Nazareth." Nathanael said to him, "Can anything good come out of Nazareth?" Philip said to him, "Come and see." When Jesus saw Nathanael coming toward him, he said of him, "Here is truly an Israelite in whom there is no deceit!" Nathanael asked him, "Where did you get to know me?" Jesus answered, "I saw you under the fig tree before Philip called you." Nathanael replied, "Rabbi, you are the Son of God! You are the King of Israel!" (John 1:43-51)

Every year, just before Easter, there is a new movie, book, or magazine article about Jesus. It never fails. You can mark your calendar. And next year, I guarantee you they'll be another movie, book, or article about Jesus. This year the offering is, *The Son of God* and Hollywood wants you come and see. Actually Hollywood wants you to come and spend. For around ten dollars for the movie, plus four dollars for popcorn, and five dollars for a soda you can go and see, *The Son of God.* People will go and watch a two hour movie about Jesus and come to Church next Sunday and tell me how wonderful the movie was and then I'll tell you that you could have stayed home and saved your twenty dollars and opened a big black book which you have on your coffee table which you probably don't read. I know because we had one of those big black books on our coffee table too when I was young and it just sat there. But you won't read the Bible and Hollywood knows that you won't. You'll go and see *The Son of God* just as you saw *The Passion of the Christ* before that and *Jesus of Montreal* before that and *Jesus Christ Superstar* before that and *The Greatest Story Ever Told* before that and on and on and on.

While on the treadmill in the local gym I watched an interview from a few movie producers from the movie and they said they had several focus groups watch the movie to make sure that no particular group of people would find the movie offensive. They invited some local Jewish rabbis' to watch the movie and make sure that Jesus wasn't too Christian so that the movie wouldn't offend the Jews. Then they invited a bunch of Christian pastors in to watch the film to make sure that Jesus wasn't too Jewish in order not to offend Christians. Then they invited women leaders to watch the film to make sure Jesus wasn't a misogynist and offend women.

The last time I read that big black book I learned that Jesus offended everyone. He offended his own disciples. When he was going to Jerusalem Peter said no Lord you can't go you have to stay with us. Jesus rebuked him by saying get behind me Satan, you have no idea what I'm supposed to be doing. He offended his own cousin John the Baptist. When John was in prison he was unsure whether or not Jesus was the real deal and sent his disciples to Jesus and Jesus said you tell John are the dead raised, do the blind see, do the deaf hear, can the lame walk? He even offended the Romans and the Jewish leaders too. Jesus offended just about everyone and anyone whom he meets. Yet Hollywood still invites us to come and see.

The Church also invites us to come and see. Every Sunday we are invited to come and meet Jesus. We meet him each week in the gospel. We meet him in the sermon. We meet him in the Eucharist. We meet him at coffee hour. We meet him in the faces of the broken and the hurt. We meet him in the stranger. We meet him in the pains and the wounds of those around us. We meet him in those who are in prison.

Meeting Jesus is exciting. When Philip meets Jesus he is so thrilled that he runs and tells his friend Nathaniel to come and see, come and see. Philip is like a kindergartner on the first day of school. The world will always tell us to come and see on the big screen or in the latest book, or in the latest magazine or newspaper article, yet for centuries, the Church reminds us that it is here where we learn who Jesus is and how faith in him can change our lives.

Food For Thought

1. Our invitation to "Come and see" leads into Jesus' invitation to "Follow me." Do we follow these two basic principles? If not, how can we hear and see better in order to see and follow?

2. Discipleship is a relational, it is person to person. Notice that Jesus called Philip and Philip called Nathaniel. In another gospel lesson Jesus called Peter and Peter went and got Andrew. The Christian message grew by sharing

the message with other people in small intimate ways, not in massive movements.

3. Read: Jeremiah 29:11, 2 Peter 1:10, Acts 2:38

Chapter Eighteen

Good News in Nazareth

In the sixth month the angel Gabriel was sent by God to a town in Galilee called Nazareth, to a virgin engaged to a man whose name was Joseph, of the house of David. The virgin's name was Mary. And he came to her and said, "Greetings, favored one! The Lord is with you." But she was much perplexed by his words and pondered what sort of greeting this might be. The angel said to her, "Do not be afraid, Mary, for you have found favor with God. And now, you will conceive in your womb and bear a son, and you will name him Jesus. He will be great, and will be called the Son of the Most High, and the Lord God will give to him the throne of his ancestor David. He will reign over the house of Jacob forever, and of his kingdom there will be no end." Mary said to the angel, "How can this be, since I am a virgin?" The angel said to her, "The Holy Spirit will come upon you, and the power of the Most High will overshadow you; therefore the child to be born will be holy; he will be called Son of God. (Luke 1:26-35)

Nazareth was a small village in the middle of nowhere. Biblical scholars say that in the first century there were only a few dozen peasants in the village: shepherds, farmers, and day laborers. Yet it's in this small village in the middle of nowhere where Jesus was born. The angel Gabriel brought Mary the good news. This news went through her ears, into her brain, then into her heart, and lodged in her womb. Nine months from today we celebrate the feast of Christmas, the birth of the Word of God. In Church Tradition Mary has been called the

Theotokos the God-bearer since she bore the Word made flesh.

The Annunciation is not an historical event, not some nice celebration of yesteryear, but it is lived and re-lived in our lives. Every time we come to Church and hear the Word of God, the Word, like Mary, goes through our ears, into our brain, then lodges in our hearts where hopefully it grows and bears fruit. However, if you're like me, sometimes that word goes in one ear and out the other. We get distracted. We don't listen. We don't care. We get cold. We forget. Yet every time we come and hear the gospel that word is planted just like a seed.

Every October I buy a bag of fifty daffodils and plant them in my front yard hoping that in March and April they'll bloom. In November and December I see squirrels and chipmunks digging in the dirt trying to find those bulbs. They're looking for their supper. If everything goes well many bulbs will stay in the ground and will send up nice green leaves but no blooms. Other bulbs barely send shoots up through the dirt. If I'm lucky I'll get a few that survive the winter and send up lovely green shoots and yellow and white blooms.

The Word of God is like those daffodil bulbs. Every time we go to Church one of those daffodil bulbs is planted in us. Week after week, year after year the Word is planted in our ears and hopefully it will find its home in our hearts where it will take root and blossom.

Food For Thought

1. Sunday mornings are often distracting. We hear crying babies, watch toddlers tumbling around the carpet and pews, and folks walking in late. We might miss the Gospel reading because folks are coughing, sneezing, or whispering to their neighbor. We miss the seeds that are planted each week. Next time you attend Church make sure to pay attention to the Word of God. Those words are not just any words but they are seeds being planted in your heart that one day will bear fruit.

2. Planting and farming depend on a lot of things out of our control. When a farmer plants corn he can only plant and hope that the corn gets enough water and sun and that the birds don't eat the corn kernels after he plants them. He cannot control the sun or the water but must live in patient hope and expectation, waiting for the harvest in late summer. A big part of our spiritual life is waiting in hope.

3. Read: John 1:46, Luke 4:16-21, Matthew 2:1-13

Chapter Nineteen

Being Available

"When Jesus had finished these parables, he left that place. He came to his hometown and began to teach the people in their synagogue, so that they were astounded and said, "Where did this man get this wisdom and these deeds of power? Is not this the carpenter's son? Is not his mother called Mary? And are not his brothers James and Joseph and Simon and Judas? And are not all his sisters with us? Where then did this man get all this?" And they took offense at him. But Jesus said to them, "Prophets are not without honor except in their own country and in their own house." And he did not do many deeds of power there, because of their unbelief." (Matthew 13:53-58)

When folks ask me what I do for a living I usually stand there for a moment wondering what I should tell them. When you ask a builder he tells you that he builds decks and tree houses. If you ask a contractor he'll tell you that he builds homes. If you ask an accountant what he does he'll tell you that he prepares tax returns. If you ask a surgeon he'll tell you that he performs surgeries.

Most people have jobs that can be quantified. A surgeon can say that he performed three surgeries last week. An accountant can tell you that he prepared twenty tax returns. A builder says that he built two decks and a tree house this week. A contractor can tell you that he built two homes this year. But what does a pastor do? Actually pastors do a variety of things: answer email, prepare sermons, meet with new members, mingle with parishioners at coffee hour, and coordinate events. I also spend a lot of time eating with people.

Matthew says that Jesus, like Joseph, was a carpenter. The Greek word is ambiguous and it could also mean that he was a stonemason. Needless to say both mean that Jesus worked with his hands. He built things. In the ancient world a carpenter would build chariots or assemble wagon wheels or frame barns. A stonemason would help construct roads or build temples. Yet not once in the gospels do we get a glimpse of what Jesus did. We hear nothing about building chariots or barns or roads or temples. Not once do we get any idea that Jesus built anything. Nothing. Nada. Zilch. I find that very interesting that Jesus didn't produce anything.

You might say to yourself: he performed miracles, right? Sure, he performed a lot of miracles but most of the time the gospels say that Jesus talks a lot. I mean a lot! From chapter five through seven all Jesus does is talk, talk, and talk. The Sermon on the Mount is one long speech.

Not only did Jesus talk a lot but he also ate a lot too. At the wedding feast at Cana of Galilee Jesus changed water into wine. And what do you do at weddings? Eat and drink. When Jesus went to Jericho and met Zacchaeus, what did Jesus do? Eat and drink. When Jesus went to Mary and Martha's house what did Jesus do? Eat and drink. When Jesus went to Bethany to raise Lazarus from the dead what did he do afterwards? Eat and drink.

After reading all of this we can say that Jesus was available to people. According to the Scriptures our God is not some foreign or strange God, our God is not remote or removed from us, but he becomes available to us in the person of Jesus.

There was a family who was divorced. The parents had a few children. One day the wife came home and told the son that his dad had purchased tickets to the local NFL football game. The dad wanted to make it a special day and have hot dogs, soda, and time together with his son. The mom told her son all of this and she was thrilled that he was going to go out on a special date together and the son said, "Nah, I don't want to." "Don't want to?" She questioned. "Why should I? He hasn't been around much. I don't feel like I really know him, why should I go to the game?" And with that the boy walked out of the room. He didn't go to the game with his dad.

Matthew invites us to become available to others. But it's hard to be available isn't it? We get distracted. We have our plans. We have our projects. We have work. We have family. We have errands. We have life. Yet being available to someone is the basis for our love of the neighbor; to listen to their pain, to be with them in crisis. To comfort them when they're sick. To rejoice when they rejoice and to laugh when they laugh. Being a Christian means being in community and this means that we're available to others even when it may be inconvenient.

Food For Thought

1. Jesus was available to people. He spent time with them in their homes, in the market, in the

synagogue, and in the farms and fields. Jesus ate with people and walked with them. Jesus opened up his life to the "other" whether they were men or women, Roman soldiers or slaves, Jewish leaders or poor peasants. Jesus practiced radical hospitality. Do you practice radical hospitality? Do you make your life available to other people? Do you welcome those who are different than you?

2. Sometimes there are a lot of distractions during the day. I could be in the middle of a project or working on a book and the phone rings or I receive an important email. I often get mad that my daily activity gets interrupted. However, later on, I realize that these little distractions or interruptions are ways that open me up to the pain or joy of someone who needs me. I try to look at these interruptions in a new light, trying to see God's hand working in my life.

3. Read: John 1:1, Romans 8:28, 1 Thessalonians 5:24

Chapter Twenty

Loving the Neighbor

"When the Son of Man comes in his glory, and all the angels with him, then he will sit on the throne of his glory. All the nations will be gathered before him, and he will separate people one from another as a shepherd separates the sheep from the goats, and he will put the sheep at his right hand and the goats at the left. Then the king will say to those at his right hand, 'Come, you that are blessed by my Father, inherit the kingdom prepared for you from the foundation of the world; for I was hungry and you gave me food, I was thirsty and you gave me something to drink, I was a stranger and you welcomed me, I was naked and you gave me clothing, I was sick and you took care of me, I was in prison and you visited me.' (Matthew 25)

There was a large congregation in a medium sized city which had a traditional downtown Main Street with a beauty parlor, bridal shop, bookstore, local library and hardware store. The parish sat at the corner of Main Street and they needed a new pastor. One day a pastor saw the advertisement for the opening. He called the parish secretary and said that he would like to apply for the position. He would come and visit the parish for two Sundays and look around for housing and schools for his children.

Both he and his wife loved the parish. It was a historical parish and it had a traditional bell tower in front and a wooden hand painted sign. They also had a brand new oak pulpit and the pastor was excited knowing that he could be preaching from it. Behind the pulpit was a brass pipe organ. They also had a large fellowship hall and playground for the children. The parish had presence and permanence.

The pastor arrived in town and preached on his first Sunday there. He loved the choir and parishioners were warm and welcoming. He delivered a very good sermon. Later that week he and his wife spent time looking around town. They enjoyed shopping and looking at schools. Towards the end of the week the pastor stopped at a Goodwill store and bought a pair of old whitewashed blue jeans that were thin and a little raggedy at the bottom. He also bought a red and black lumberjack over shirt and an old pair of sneakers that had holes in them. On the way home he stopped at a costume shop and bought a brown beard that would match his hair color.

The following Sunday the pastor dressed in his new outfit. He arrived about an hour early and sat across the sidewalk from the Church so members of the congregations would have to pass by him in order to go inside. He had a makeshift sign that read, "Need Help" and held an empty coffee cup. He didn't talk to anyone. He just sat there.

After about an hour lying across the front steps he secretly walked into the Church office, removed his fake beard, combed his hair, put on his preaching robes, and lead worship. It was a beautiful service, the choir was excellent and his sermon was good. At the end of the service the pastor delivered the announcements and said that if he were to accept the position of head pastor he would, but there was one condition. He quickly turned around, took off his preaching robes and faced the congregation. There was a quiet hush. He then said, "This morning I sat in front of the parish for about an hour or so before the services. How many people from this parish do you think stopped and helped me?" There was a slight pause and then someone raised their hand and said, "Eighty percent." "Wrong," the pastor said. Then another person raised their hand, "I think about fifty percent." "Wrong again," the pastor said. Finally someone near the front raised their hand and said, "Well, I think that at least a third of us stopped to help." "Wrong again." Then the pastor responded, "I sat for an hour in front of this Church and only three of you stopped to give me anything." He continued, "The sign on your building says Holy Spirit Church, well this is not a Church. This is a club, this is a fellowship, this is a group, this is not different than the Rotary or the Kiwanis, but this is not a Church. According to the Book of Acts the early Christians met on the first day of the week for the breaking of the bread and the prayers which is the Eucharist, for fellowship, and that they held everything in common and helped one another and those in need. Well, you have the first two done but not the third. If you are willing to do the third then I will come and be your pastor. If you won't, then you need to look for someone else." The pastor then stepped down from the pulpit, changed out of his Goodwill clothes and went and visited with the parishioners at the coffee fellowship. During coffee fellowship the members of the congregation talked among themselves and said that they still wanted him as their pastor and that they'd start doing outreach programs. They wanted to change their lives.

The same thing happened to me when I arrived at my parish. Although my parish certainly wasn't a historical Church and I didn't dress up like a homeless man, we still had our problems. When I arrived the congregation they had the weekly Divine Liturgy, they had fellowship, but they had no outreach programs. After preaching for a few months about the necessity of loving the neighbor a parishioner stopped me after the Sunday service and suggested that we have a prayer breakfast on the following Saturday morning in order to discuss the future of the parish. We had pancakes, eggs, sausage, bacon, and coffee. The person said we are not going to leave until we decided on an outreach ministry. He was tired of just going to Church and taking communion. So we talked and debated and we wanted to choose something that we would do well, that we would do consistently, that we would succeed at. We decided to adopt the Men's Rescue Mission as our first ministry. It would cost us one hundred and fifty dollars to serve a hot lunch for one hundred men. And we did that. For fourteen years we have been serving a hot lunch once a month for a hundred men. After we were doing that for a while someone else approached me at coffee hour and said, "Father, I get more out of this than the guys do, I feel much more love for service and for my faith."

When we read Matthew's version of the final judgment we shouldn't be shocked. We shouldn't say, "Gee this is something new." Jesus' last words to his disciples and to us are a constant reminder of what we should be doing all the time, loving those around us no matter if they're black, white, or brown, whether they speak English or Spanish or French, whether they are young or old. Matthew's message is clear. The final judgment is not based on how much we donate to the building fund or how many candles we light or how many prayers we say or what we do for a living. Our judgment will be based on loving those around us.

Food For Thought

1. Attending Sunday worship is easy, but it's only a very small part of our faith. Faith requires action, it involves getting ourselves deep and dirty helping those in need. There are so many ways, both big and small, that we can help other people. We can donate food to the local food bank. We can help cook and serve a hot meal to homeless people. We can donate our time to a local charity. We can write a check to someone who needs help. The list is endless, just as our love for the neighbor should be endless.

2. Jesus devoted his life to the poor. He welcomed the stranger. He was open to the hurt and the homeless. Take some time out of your day and think and pray about those who are less fortunate than you are. Think of those who have no bed tonight, who only have enough food for one meal, who cannot afford a house or an

apartment. Make your prayer for the poor a regular part of your prayer routine and reflection and see where it leads you.

3. Read: Proverbs 25:17-18, James 2:8, Matthew 19:16-18

Chapter Twenty-One

Running From God

Now the word of the Lord came to Jonah son of Amittai, saying, "Go at once to Nineveh, that great city, and cry out against it; for their wickedness has come up before me." But Jonah set out to flee to Tarshish from the presence of the Lord. He went down to Joppa and found a ship going to Tarshish; so he paid his fare and went on board, to go with them to Tarshish, away from the presence of the Lord. (Jonah 1:1-3)

Monica was a recent college graduate and she was lucky to land a job immediately after graduation. She was an accounting major and found a job at the local bank. She liked her boss and co-workers. After she was there for a few weeks she was upset at her boss. He would offer helpful hints for Monica to be a better accountant. Monica didn't like it so much. She eventually found a job at another bank.

As Monica was looking for a new job she also began dating. Monica's mom was happy because now she had a new job, was paying her own rent, car payments, and student loans. She assumed that Monica would soon be married. She dated a few guys and most of her friends were jealous because most of the guys were very smart, they paid for lunch or dinner, and one guy even brought her flowers. Yet Monica always found something wrong with them. One guy had too much hair, one guy hardly had any hair at all. One guy had an earing and the other guy had a bunch of tattoos. She eventually dumped them. Her friends thought she was crazy. Her mom thought she was crazy too.

Her mom told her, "You know Monica, maybe you need a change of scenery? You know, new city, new job, new boyfriend—a fresh start, a new beginning." She agreed. So she packed her bags and moved to Virginia. She was happy. After settling in she got a job right away at yet another bank and started dating. But guess what happened? She had trouble at work again and she dumped her boyfriend. Her mom said, "You know Monica, maybe the problem isn't work or the guys you're dating. Maybe the problem is you." After a moment of silence Monica said, "You know mom, maybe you're right. I'm going to get some help." Monica went to a therapist and after a few sessions she realized that her problems were in her head and in her heart. She realized that she was running away from something. Now she had to find out what that something was.

The story of Jonah and the whale is a story of running away. When I was young my parents read me the Jonah story. When you read it again as an adult you see the violence and emotion in the story which people often glance over when reading the story as a child. God calls Jonah to preach to the Ninevites, and from what we gather they were a bad bunch of folks. They didn't follow God's teachings. So God asked Jonah to preach to them. Jonah didn't want to, so he headed for the harbor to find a ship that was headed for Tarsish. Biblical scholars tell us that Tarshish another way of saying Spain. In other words Jonah was headed in the opposite direction of Nineveh.

After a while the sea stormed and since Jonah believed in God the sailors wanted to throw him into the sea. They did. Most of us think that God commanded a large fish to swallow Jonah, but the original wording doesn't say fish, it says whale or sea monster as in a big humpback whale. After three days the whale vomited Jonah on the beach. Jonah learned something after that experience and started preaching. The story continues and in some ways the ending is more interesting than the beginning. Yet the striking thing is that when God asked Jonah to go to Nineveh he headed in the opposite direction.

This seems to be a common theme in the Bible. In Genesis, after Adam and Eve ate from the tree of the knowledge of Good and Evil God went looking for Adam saying, "Adam, where are you?" After Adam and Eve ate the fruit their eyes were opened and they realized that they were disobedient to God. Their gut reaction was to run away. Jeremiah had the same problem. When God sent Jeremiah to preach to the Israelites Jeremiah said, "But I'm only a youth." He wanted to run away too, but Jeremiah was smarter than Jonah, he listened to God.

When I was in high school I wanted to run away too. I hated my parents, hated them with a capital H. I was angry. I slammed the door and had a green army duffle bag that I packed with some clothes. But I was too chicken to go through with it. I knew that kids did run away and many lived at the train station or bus stop or under the parkway, they were the brave ones. I was too scared to actually go through with it so I stayed home.

Running From God

Running away is tempting. Folks want to run away from their spouses, from their children, from their jobs. When the going gets tough we are tempted to run away. Hopefully this time we won't.

Food For Thought

1. Was there a time in your life when you felt like you wanted to run away? What was the situation? How did you deal with it?

2. We often get angry at God because we don't want to deal with life as it is. We want to run away from life like we want to run away from Him. Rather than running away from God we perhaps need to run towards Him, to embrace Him with open arms.

3. Read: 2 Chronicles 16:11, Hebrews 10:36, Galatians 6:9

Chapter Twenty-Two

Having Jesus Eyes

"As he was setting out on a journey, a man ran up and knelt before him, and asked him, "Good Teacher, what must I do to inherit eternal life?" Jesus said to him, "Why do you call me good? No one is good but God alone. You know the commandments: 'You shall not murder; You shall not commit adultery; You shall not steal; You shall not bear false witness; You shall not defraud; Honor your father and mother.'" He said to him, "Teacher, I have kept all these since my youth." Jesus, looking at him, loved him and said, "You lack one thing; go, sell what you own, and give the money to the poor, and you will have treasure in heaven; then come, follow me." When he heard this, he was shocked and went away grieving, for he had many possessions." (Mark 10:17-31)

A while ago I was having trouble reading. Every time I'd look at my email or read a book I'd get headaches. I noticed that the headaches and my eyestrain didn't go away. I went to the eye doctor and she asked me what was going on. She said that I probably needed glasses. Glasses? No way. I was fine. I thought I was having computer problems, not eye problems. I was in denial. Some folks are in denial about their eyes, others about their hearing, and others for other things. She gave me an eye test and sure enough I needed glasses.

The same thing happened with my windshield wipers. I noticed that my windshield would often get foggy. I had my car checked out and everything was fine. I took my car in for an oil change and they guy told me that you need your wipers changed. They cost around twenty dollars. I said no way, twenty dollars is too much. So I drove the car as it was. But it wasn't getting any better. Matter of fact it got worse, much worse. After a while I went to one of those quick oil change places and they said that we'll change the wiper blades for fifteen dollars and voila, I could see again. Crazy. Just a simple thing but it changed the way that I saw the world.

All of us view the world through our eyes. We see the world see unique cultural or ethnic backgrounds, according to our various political contexts, according to our geographic upbringing.

We are invited to see the world through the eyes of Jesus, to see the world with Jesus eyes means to see the world as he sees it. How does this work you may ask? Well, a lady came to me once complaining about her sister. She said, "Father, twenty years ago my sister and I had a great big fight at Thanksgiving. She made a rude comment about my cooking and the way that I raised my children. I got mad at her and haven't spoken to her since."

I stood there in amazement. Clearly this woman was angry. She even told me, I'm never going to forgive her. In the eyes of the world she has every right to act this way. But doesn't Jesus say that we need to forgive others? Doesn't he say that we are to forgive others up to seventy times seven? Doesn't he say that if you and your brother have anything against you that you should go and reconcile before going up to the Temple?

Then there was a guy who once told me, "You know Father, why should I give money to the poor, after all my tax money goes for Medicaid and libraries and roads, I pay enough in taxes so why should I give extra?" I stood there and thought, you know, he's right. We pay property tax, gas tax, school tax, state tax, sales tax, and cigarette tax. Those taxes help pay for public works projects, for schools, roads, food stamps, and Medicare and Medicaid. But doesn't Jesus say render what is Caesars unto Caesar and God what is God's? Doesn't he say that we are supposed to help the poor and for our left hand not to know what our right hand is doing? In the eyes of the world the man is perfectly right, but in the eyes of Jesus he is off the mark.

Finally there was the guy who told me right after 9/11 happened that we should just carpet bomb Iraq, make it a parking lot. Drop a nuclear bomb and just flatten the whole place and start again. We can go in there and give them more money, resources, funds, and so forth and we can build the country up again, build new schools, roads, hospitals, and start fresh. When I asked him about all the innocent men, women, and children who weren't fighting his response was, oh, that's the price of war, it's called collateral damage. He's right too. We did the same thing in Nagasaki and Hiroshima and we could do it again. It worked in Japan so it should work in Iraq too. And what about all of those innocent people?

Yet in the eyes of Jesus we know that's so far off base. Doesn't Jesus say bless those who curse you and love your enemies? The man said, "But..." But what? Jesus isn't offering us opinions about life; he's showing us what true life is about, yet we usually choose the opposite.

Food For Thought

1. The rich man had many possessions and he had a hard time letting them go. Do you have thing things in your life that you cannot let go? Why do you think this is?

2. Following Jesus isn't always easy. It's downright hard sometime. If you are struggling with your faith take one day at a time.

3. Read: Matthew 6:19-21, Luke 12:15, 1 Timothy 6:10

Chapter Twenty-Three

God's Big Crazy Family

"An account of the genealogy of Jesus the Messiah, the son of David, the son of Abraham. Abraham was the father of Isaac, and Isaac the father of Jacob, and Jacob the father of Judah and his brothers, and Judah the father of Perez and Zerah by Tamar, and Perez the father of Hezron, and Hezron the father of Aram, and Aram the father of Aminadab, and Aminadab the father of Nahshon, and Nahshon the father of Salmon, and Salmon the father of Boaz by Rahab, and Boaz the father of Obed by Ruth, and Obed the father of Jesse, and Jesse the father of King David." (Matthew 1:1-6)

Because I'm a pastor I hear a lot of complaints from parishioners. These complaints aren't about neighbors or friends or co-workers, these complaints are usually about family members. I hear about brothers who fight with brothers, sisters who fight with sisters, grandparents who don't visit enough and grandparents who visit too much. I hear about former family fights and jealousies and people who withhold love. I hear about Uncle Stanley who always gets drunk at Christmas but no one admits it. I hear about the sister who never comes to family gatherings because she and her mom don't get along. I've heard it all. We may think our are families are normal. We put on a good face, but deep down all of us have families that are messed up.

Up until about age ten I used to think I had the perfect family. I grew up watching the Partridge Family and the Brady Bunch and the Jefferson's and Family Ties. I said,

"Those families are strange." Then I looked around at my friends' families and said, "Those families are strange." Then I looked at my own family and said, "Oh my gosh. My family is crazier than the rest of them." But it's true; we live with crazies and crackpots most of the time.

When reading the gospels we often forget that Jesus had a family. We know that he wasn't married and didn't have children of his own but he had a large extended family. We know that Mary and Joseph were his parents and that according to Tradition Joachim and Anna were his grandparents. John the Baptist was his cousin and Elizabeth and Zechariah were his uncle and aunt. He also had a host of family members; Abraham, Sarah, Noah, David, Tamar, and others. Please don't think that these people were perfect because they weren't. The Bible doesn't cover it up either, they leave all the dirty laundry out there to be seen by all.

When the Angel Gabriel visited Mary telling her that she was going to have a child, do you think that Joseph wanted to pass out cigars and have a party? No. He wanted to run the other way. What about Zechariah? He wasn't much different than Joseph. When Gabriel came to him telling him that in nine months he'd have a son he said, "No way, this ain't going to happen." God said I'll fix his wagon so he made Zechariah dumb for nine months and he couldn't talk. The rest of Jesus' family wasn't any better; David was a murderer, Tamar was a prostitute, Noah got drunk, and Sarah doubted God. When an angel came to her saying that in nine months when he returns she would have a baby she said, No way, I'm a great-great-grandma, I'm not giving birth to a baby." God said yes you will and in nine months she gave birth to Isaac which in Hebrew means, she who laughs. If you still think your family is perfect you are dead wrong.

When new people come to my parish they often think that these are perfect. But one day they'll come to Church on a Sunday morning and they'll think my sermon is boring or that I'm cold to them at coffee hour. They may come and they'll be only three people in the choir and it will sound rather sour. And maybe that Sunday rather than a big spread for coffee hour we'll just have chips and salsa and maybe a few cookies. Far from perfect if you ask me. But that's how life is isn't it. I tell folks if you come looking for a perfect parish you got the wrong place.

We don't come to Church because it's a perfect place we come to Church because we are on our way to perfection. We haven't arrived yet. We're on our way. Jesus says in the gospels, be perfect as your father is perfect. How do we become perfect? We become perfect by hearing the Word of God and keeping it. We become perfect by coming to Sunday services and hearing the sermon and sharing fellowship with one another. We become perfect by loving and serving our neighbor. We become perfect by following God's commandments and doing his will. No, we're not perfect yet, but we're all on our way to perfection and I hope we can all get there in one piece.

Food For Thought

1. Take some time and think about your family. Do you have a crazy cast of characters that drive you nuts? If so, who are they? Why do they drive you crazy?

2. Jesus tells us to be perfect as our heavenly father is perfect. Do you try to be perfect? Do you strive to do good all the time? If not, why not?

3. Read: Matthew 5:48, Colossians 3:20, 1 Timothy 3:5

Chapter Twenty-Four

We're Not Alone

"Soon afterwards he went to a town called Nain, and his disciples and a large crowd went with him. As he approached the gate of the town, a man who had died was being carried out. He was his mother's only son, and she was a widow; and with her was a large crowd from the town. When the Lord saw her, he had compassion for her and said to her, "Do not weep." Then he came forward and touched the bier, and the bearers stood still. And he said, "Young man, I say to you, rise!" The dead man sat up and began to speak, and Jesus gave him to his mother. Fear seized all of them; and they glorified God, saying, "A great prophet has risen among us!" and "God has looked favorably on his people!" This word about him spread throughout Judea and all the surrounding country." (Luke 7:11-17)

Throughout the year I usually get a call from someone who is a Christian but who doesn't attend a parish and who may need some prayers or some assistance. Recently someone called wanting me to make a pastoral visit to a dying relative.

The man was in his early nineties and like many elderly people he fell and broke a hip and needed a hip replacement. He couldn't return home right away so he was sent to the assisted care facility and he left with more than a hip. He left with a nasty staph infection and since he was not walking around he contracted pneumonia. Now the guy had a nice new hip but was in really bad shape. Since his health was compromised he was then sent to hospice care. That's where I visited him. I heard his confession, said a few prayers, and gave him communion. He died later that week.

While driving home I thought how lucky this guy was. I know you may think that's crazy but in a way he was really lucky. He had two children to arrange for his operation, they called his insurance company and then the social security office. They helped feed him and visited him and gave him his medications. Even though he was very sick he had someone in charge of his care. Taking care of someone is really hard and many times it's like having a part time job.

What happens to an elderly person who lives alone in the middle of nowhere and has an emergency? Who arranges for the rehab center or clinic? Who calls the insurance and the social security department or the pharmacy? Who arranges for physical therapy or contacts Medicare? When you have a major illness, especially a life threatening one it's overwhelming. You may think, well, isn't that what the social worker is supposed to do? Yes it is their job but have you ever seen a social worker's desk? It's piled a mile high with reports and papers and patient information. As the saying goes the squeaky wheel gets the grease. If the patient isn't complaining or whining they're not going to be a high priority. I know it sounds crazy but it's true. Being alone in time of great need is terrible.

The widow in Luke's gospel felt pretty alone that day as she was headed out of Nain to bury her son. She had no one. No husband and probably no brother or sister either. Who was going to be with her in her time of need? During the time of Jesus a widow was literally at the bottom of society. You couldn't go much lower than a widow. Yet she wasn't alone. No. Because on that day as the funeral procession was passing through a man stopped the funeral procession and changed her life. His name was Jesus. Yes, Jesus. He saw the procession and stopped it and asked the woman why are you weeping? He then said, "Child arise," and the boy got up. Jesus changed her life. No longer was she alone with no one to care. Jesus was there. He cared. He cared so much for her that he brought her son back to life. She was no longer alone, isolated, and grieving.

There might be times when we're all alone too. Times when we feel isolated and lonely, times when we're in darkness and despair. Yet like the widow of Nain we're not alone. Like this lonely widow we have Jesus. We have Jesus and so does the rest of the world but they don't know it. Jesus cares because he was alone. He was thrown out of Nazareth. He was chased out of town by the Pharisees. He was hounded by King Herod. He was thrown into jail by Pontius Pilate. Jesus was very much alone and this is why he cares for us.

That day in Nain he showed compassion to this widow and it changed her life. He shows compassion on us and it changes our life. We turn and share this compassion with others and it changes their life too.

Food For Thought

1. Were there times in your life when you felt all alone? What were the circumstances? How did you get through this terrible time?

2. Many parishes have a visitation ministry. If someone is in the hospital or at home sick parishioners will go visit them. People appreciate a visit and prayers. If your parish has a visitation ministry I encourage you to participate in it. This will make the person feel connected to the community even though they cannot attend services regularly.

3. Read: Genesis 2:18, John 10:27, Romans 8:35-39

Chapter Twenty-Five

A Violent World

When Herod saw that he had been tricked by the wise men, he was infuriated, and he sent and killed all the children in and around Bethlehem who were two years old or under, according to the time that he had learned from the wise men. Then was fulfilled what had been spoken through the prophet Jeremiah: "A voice was heard in Ramah, wailing and loud lamentation, Rachel weeping for her children; she refused to be consoled, because they are no more." (Mathew 2: 16-18)

Currently there is an ongoing debate about whether or not movies, television, and certain video games cause violent behavior or that movies, television, and video games reflect a violent society.I know when I was young I saw plenty of horror movies and watched television shows that I probably shouldn't have watched and played video games and I turned out okay. I didn't wind up in jail, or become a robber, or stab anyone. Yet plenty of folks do. I'm not a psychologist or sociologist, but my two cents is that bad television programs, movies, and violent video games reflect our culture, because indeed we are a violent bunch.

Some library systems are considering putting rating on books like they have ratings on movies: G for general audience, PG for parental guidance, PG-13 for children under 13, R for no one under 17 or 18, and NR for adults only. Yet one book that we all probably have in our homes should be rated NR and that is the Bible. The Bible is a very violent book yet we often don't realize it.

A Violent World

In the Exodus story God sends a series of plagues to attack the Egyptians; all the rivers and streams turned to blood, locusts and frogs destroyed all the vegetation. God sent the angel of death to kill all the first-born children. Then later when the Israelites crossed safely through the Red Sea to the Promised Land, all the soldiers and their horses died in the rushing waters. Later in the Bible David killed Goliath with a slingshot. Jonah was swallowed by a whale. John the Baptist had his head chopped off. Stephen was stoned, Paul was beaten and put into jail, and then of course Jesus was arrested and crucified.

And in the very beginning of the gospel story, a wonderful, beautiful, joyful, story, the story of the birth of Jesus with the angels announcing the good news, the visit of the shepherds, the visit of the wise men, the Virgin Mary and Joseph holding the Christ child, at the very center of this happy occasion is violence. Seven miles up the road from Bethlehem in his palace near the Temple sat King Herod with all his power, and all his money, and all his soldiers and he went into a violent rage. He was angry and jealous because of a little baby; the prince of peace, the king of the Jews was born. He was so jealous that he had his soldiers kill all the male children who were two and under. Fast forward the story twenty-six chapters and you have Pontius Pilate the Roman governor sitting in his palace having to deal with an adult Jesus, the king of the Jews. Pilate, like King Herod wanted Jesus dead.

I was never sent to jail or was arrested or hit anyone yet I certainly killed plenty of people with my words. I certainly thought very bad thoughts about people. I certainly wished people harm. Where does this all come from? It all comes from my heart. I know that when I'm angry it starts in my heart. I know that when I'm mad it starts in my heart. I know that when I feel rage it starts in my heart.

You may be thinking to yourself what's the point? Who cares? Why bother. Yet Mohandas Gandhi changed India not with authority, power, soldiers, or tanks but with his heart. When he had love or forgiveness or mercy in his heart others around him had love and mercy and forgiveness in their hearts too. The same goes for Martin Luther King. He changed our country not with power or authority or money or soldiers but with his heart. When he had love in his heart and mercy in his heart or forgiveness in his heart others around him had love and mercy and forgiveness in their hearts too. And what did Jesus do? He didn't change the world with power or authority or soldiers or money. No. He had love and mercy and forgiveness in his heart.

We can change the world. We can change ourselves. We can change the world around us but we have to stat with our hearts. If our heart is in the right place then we can make the world a better place.

Food For Thought

1. Have there been times in your life when you feel anger, rage, or violence. Are there times in your life when you have thought bad thoughts about others? Each of us is capable of great evil. We

always must keep our anger in check, otherwise it may take over.

2. In the Sermon on the Mount we read, "Blessed are the peacemakers for they shall be called sons of God." (Matthew 5:9). The more we can bring peace and love into the world the better.

3. Read: Isaiah 12:2, Philippians 4:6, Romans 12:18

Recommended Reading

Enzo Bianchi. *Praying the Word: An Introduction to Lectio Divina.* Kalamazoo, MI: Cistercian Publications, 1998.

Raymond E. Brown. *Christ in the Gospels of the Liturgical Year (Expanded Edition With Essays).* Collegeville, MN: The Liturgical Press, 2008.

James Martin. *Between Heaven and Mirth: Why Joy, Humor, and Laughter Are at the Heart of the Spiritual Life.* NY: Harper One, 2011.

-------------- *Becoming Who You Are.* Mahwah, NJ: Hidden Spring Books, 2006.

William C. Mills. *Encountering Jesus in the Gospels.* Rollinsford, NH: Orthodox Research Institute, 2012.

------------------ *A 30 Day Retreat: A Personal Guide to Spiritual Renewal.* Mahwah, NJ: Paulist Press, 2010.

-----------------*Walking With God: Stories of Life and Faith.* Rollinsford, NH: Orthodox Research Institute, 2014.

Henri Nouwen. *Reading the Signs of Daily Life.* NY: Harper One, 2013.

CPSIA information can be obtained at www.ICGtesting.com
Printed in the USA
BVOW06s0007261015

423937BV00003BA/6/P